PROCESS
IMPROVEMENT

A GUIDE FOR TEAMS

SECOND
EDITION

Coopers
&Lybrand

Clifton Cooksey
Richard Beans
Debra Eshelman

Bulk quantities of this book may be obtained at a discount from

Publishing Division, Coopers & Lybrand,

1530 Wilson Blvd., Arlington, VA 22209

Phone (703) 908-1500.

Cooksey, Clifton M., Richard L. Beans, Debra L. Eshelman

Process Improvement: A Guide for Teams

Library of Congress Catalog Number 92-054917

ISBN 0-944533-06-X

Table of Contents

Acknowledgements iii

Preface v

How To Use This Guide vii

Chapter 1: Overview 1

Chapter 2: Becoming A Team 11

Chapter 3: Define The Process 29

Chapter 4: Measure Process Performance 45

Chapter 5: Identify Improvement Opportunities 69

Chapter 6: Develop Solutions 97

Chapter 7: From Recommendation To Reality 129

Toolbox 153

References...233

About the Authors 235

Index 237

ACKNOWLEDGEMENTS

Since the first edition of this book was published, we have had the opportunity to work with more than a hundred public and private sector teams. Their contribution to this edition has been immeasurable. In addition, we wish to thank Coopers & Lybrand partner Ian Littman for his unflagging support of our efforts. We also owe a debt of gratitude to Greg Gullickson and other Coopers & Lybrand consulting staff members who provided us with critical insight and assistance during the course of this project. Finally, we deeply appreciate the commitment to excellence displayed by project director Steve Clyburn, writer/editor Mary Anne Reilly, production manager Michael Clover, graphic artists Robert Bartolo, Margaret Smith, and Kimberly Farcot, word processing director Ana Fano, and word processor Lucia Gladchtein. Without such assistance, this edition would not have been possible.

Other Books by Coopers & Lybrand

BreakPoint Business Process Redesign (1993)

Excellence in Government:

Total Quality Management in the 1990s

Second Edition (1993)

Measuring Quality:

Linking Customer Satisfaction to Process Improvement

(1993)

PREFACE

We wrote this book because we believe that you and others directly involved in the process of getting things done in your organization — whether you take an order, receive an invoice, or ship merchandise to customers — know more about what causes problems in these areas than anyone else in your organization. Using your knowledge of the way things are done and the processes you already follow every day, you and your teammates can show the rest of the organization how to do things more quickly, intelligently, cheaply, and easily, and more to your customer's liking than ever before.

We've designed this book to help you — and those who will be working with you — to make all of that happen. *Process Improvement: A Guide for Teams* is organized to aid any team, whether it is composed of managers or operators or both managers *and* operators, to improve the way a job gets done.

Throughout this book, we will be following the process improvement method first introduced by quality experts W. Edwards Deming and Walter J. Shewhart: the Plan-Do-Check-Act (PDCA) Cycle, one of the basic tools of quality management.

Over the years, our commitment to working with teams and using the PDCA cycle to achieve results has remained strong for one very simple reason: it works. Using PDCA with teams has worked so well, in fact, that it has begun to change the way management and the rank and file view their relationships with one another.

Back in 1989, for example, when we put together the first edition of this book, middle managers shared the responsibility of directing teamwork with virtually no one. Managers alone would determine who would serve on a team, then they asked teams to do the research needed to plan projects, decided alone whether to implement team suggestions, and supervised changes once they were made.

That is no longer the case. Successful team-based process improvement efforts have, in some places, earned such respect from management that managers are now participating in as well as leading teams. In some organizations, management has given teams made up of operators the authority to manage themselves.

If you serve on one of these *self-managed teams*, make sure that you include the management-related responsibilities we describe in the chapters ahead on your list of things to do. If you're a manager in an organization that holds management meetings without the benefit of these techniques, consider introducing them to your peers.

Finally, as you work together to improve the processes you currently use to get things done, keep this in mind: We have found that a team performs best when it also seeks and includes input from people who are not team members. When management, other employees, customers, and suppliers are shut out of your process, their ideas are, too. Take in all the information you can, and good luck!

HOW TO USE THIS GUIDE

Part 1

Part 1 introduces the concept of process improvement and discusses related topics, such as how our understanding of what "quality" really means affects customer satisfaction. This section also discusses how teams can improve organization processes, explains the Plan-Do-Check-Act (PDCA) Cycle, and shows you how to select a process to improve. It's a good idea to read this first, if you're not familiar with Total Quality Management (TQM) and the way it approaches quality improvement.

The Plan-Do-Check-Act Cycle
A Framework for Improvement

Part 2

Part 2 describes the improvement process as it is outlined in the PDCA Cycle pictured below (figure 1-1).

Read this entire section quickly to get a feel for the journey you're about to take. Don't be surprised or discouraged if you don't understand the whole process the first time around. Return to the parts you had trouble with after you've read through all of the sections. The material is better absorbed that way.

If you're a member of a team, it's strongly recommended that you and your teammates read the introductory chapter on teams, "Becoming a Team," together. To prepare themselves best for this process, teams should:

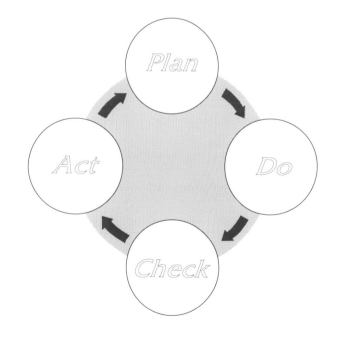

1. Read through each PDCA-related chapter together.

2. Work as a team through the activities discussed in each chapter as soon as possible after everyone has read it.

3. Repeat steps 1 and 2 throughout all of the PDCA chapters.

Part 3

This section is your "Toolbox." It holds detailed instructions about how to use the tools and techniques discussed in Part 2. Refer to the Toolbox whenever you get ready to use a tool.

References

Should you want to read more about the topics discussed in *Process Improvement*, you'll find a list of useful references in the Appendix.

Chapter 1

OVERVIEW

Have you ever played on a team whose members each understand the rules of the game a little differently? If you have, you probably realize how important it is for all team members to know what they're doing and why they're doing it before they scramble onto the field.

That's what this section of *Process Improvement* is all about. Read through Part 1 carefully — and together — and you'll reach a common understanding of what you'll be striving to achieve and why.

Quality

The first thing to bear in mind is this: the objective of process improvement is to enhance the quality of products or services by improving the processes that produce them. That can't be attempted, however, unless you ask yourselves and your customers, what quality is. Consider the following example:

Let's say that a computer hardware manufacturer designs a sleeker, sturdier PC. It's beautiful, contemporary, crafted with care by quality-minded designers — and weighs 10 pounds. The only problem is, what the manufacturer's customers really want is a lighter model — one that weighs 4 pounds. All other things being equal, the most important thing to this company's customers is weight — and, to the chagrin of this company's management, their customers will have to go elsewhere to find what they need.

In this case, customers defined quality as not necessarily the best there is, but what they wanted and needed for their particular circumstances. Keep this in mind as you plan and execute your process improvement efforts.

This is not to say that you have to wait for your customers to tell you what quality is. There are ways you can find out right away what it might mean. For instance, if you're doing things that matter — that is, producing reports that people use rather than throw away, then you're producing something of value. Quality can always be measured by the value a product or service has for your customers, both inside and outside your organization.

There are other questions you can ask yourselves that will shed light on what quality may mean to you and your customers. How well does your delivery process function? Is the product or service you offer free from defects? Is it on time? Does it cost too much? The answers to these questions can begin to show you what quality means to your customers. And they can also point out which of your organization's processes are working — and which are not.

The Bigger Picture: Total Quality Management

All of these quality- and customer-oriented process improvement ideas come under the umbrella of Total Quality Management (TQM), an approach to improving the way organizations do business that is achieving success in both the public and private sectors of the world's economy. TQM assumes that change occurs whether we want it to or not. It is a method for managing change that ensures that the changes an organization inevitably undergoes will have a positive impact on the people and processes involved.

With TQM, everyone involved, including customers and suppliers, improves the quality of products and services by analyzing and improving the processes that produce them. This requires commitment. For TQM to work, people at all levels of the organization must participate in decision-making and work effectively in teams.

By now, you're probably trying to figure out how TQM affects the nuts and bolts of everyday life. The chart on page 8 provides some clues. "What's Different Under TQM" shows how this approach can create a more positive work environment. Many employees say, for example, that coming to work in a TQM workplace is more fun and challenging than ever before.

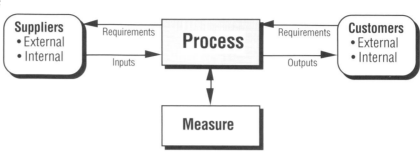

Customer-Supplier Relationship

So, are you tired of "fighting fires" instead of doing your real job? Are decisions in your organization incorrectly made because the right people don't have a say in them? Are problems transferred to another department instead of being solved because "the left hand doesn't know what the right hand is doing"? If you answered "yes" to any of these questions, then TQM is for you.

As you read through this book, keep in mind that TQM is not an overnight cure for what ails your organization — it can't be installed like a computer system. It requires management's commitment and your own full participation. Remember that, in taking part in a process improvement team, you are on your way toward helping your organization make quality management a reality.

Customers and Suppliers

Many people have been taught to think of customers as the people who receive the finished products or services — the cars, the insurance, the Social Security checks — that organizations such as yours sell or provide to them. That's partly right, of course.

But it's best to expand your point of view a bit. Why? Because thinking about work as a series of processes helps you to see that a customer is anyone who receives or uses what you produce, no matter where your work fits in the scheme of things.

A Process May Be...

SIMPLE
- Taking a photograph
- Buying a radio
- Balancing your checkbook

COMPLEX
- Developing film
- Buying a new radar system
- Balancing the federal budget

There Are Many Levels of Processes...

Some of these people are internal customers: other units or people in your organization whose part in a work process comes after yours.

You have other kinds of internal customers as well. These customers — employees who work in another department, for example — might also use your work to assist them in completing a totally different process. For instance, your organization could be getting ready to bid on a new project and need the records you keep on the current one to draw up an estimate of what it'll take to do the proposed job. These people are doing something totally different with your work, but they are internal customers nonetheless.

External customers, on the other hand, are the people most of us have traditionally viewed as customers. They can be direct customers, such as auto mechanics who order parts from a manufacturer, or indirect customers, such as the people who take their cars to those mechanics for repairs.

Now, you may ask, what about suppliers, the vendors who sell to your organization? Well, the truth of the matter is, they are customers, too. Process improvement thinking requires you to consider everyone you deal with in business as both a supplier and a customer. In other words, everyone who is working on a process is a customer to the process that precedes it and a supplier to the next process down the line.

What it all boils down to is this: Supplier-customer relationships for both internal and external customers are reciprocal. If you learn to communicate and work well together, everyone — and the processes they use — will be better off for it. Treat your suppliers like customers, and you will have better suppliers. Make sure your customers give you the right information, and you will be a better supplier. Guaranteed.

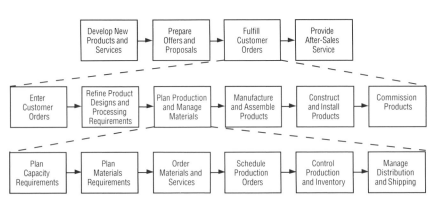

Processes and Systems

Any sequence of activities that takes place in order to get work done is a process. Processes range, in order of complexity, from something simple like writing a check, to functional, like maintaining an organization's financial records, to cross-functional, like drawing up an organization's financial plan.

Every process receives inputs — that is, material from another source, such as bills that have to be paid. Information is generally included with this material, such as an authorization to pay a bill. Once someone has received that information, a process transformation (which in this case includes all the steps involved in writing a check) can occur. That transformation, in turn, produces a product or service — the process's output.

All processes, regardless of their size or complexity, change something for somebody. Such processes, as they grow larger and involve many people and organizational departments, are often referred to as systems.

From time to time, your process improvement work may put you in touch with systems as well as processes in your organization. But it's best to remember that most of the time you'll be focusing on specific processes, since improving quality relies on the work that they do. Once you learn to view your organization as a network of processes and systems, you'll begin to see how individual and group contributions affect and are affected by the work of many others.

Measurement

Many people make decisions based on gut-level feelings about situations. There's nothing wrong with that — instincts provide insight into better ways to handle problems. Often, however, more information than just instincts is needed.

That's where quality measurement comes in. Throughout this book, you'll learn how to measure a number of things, including customer expectations, performance, and the workings of the individual

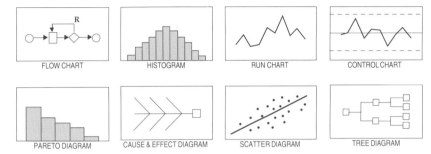

FLOW CHART HISTOGRAM RUN CHART CONTROL CHART

PARETO DIAGRAM CAUSE & EFFECT DIAGRAM SCATTER DIAGRAM TREE DIAGRAM

Quality Tools

parts of a process. These measurement techniques will provide you with objective information that will add to or balance the information you already have. They'll also make your decision-making process much easier.

There's one more thing about quality measurement you should know: Measurement is not about grading people. No one will be evaluating every move you make. Measurement techniques are used to determine how processes are performing, not people.

Variation

Virtually everything in your life varies: your weight (especially around the holidays), the amount of time it takes to drive to work, how long it takes to finish a monthly report. Some organizations view variations in performance as simply good or bad, but there's more to it than that. When the performance of a conveyor belt or software varies over time, the degree to which it varies is telling you something about what's happening to it.

Some variation is inevitable, but a high degree of variation makes processes unstable and erratic. Why? Because variation reduces the uniformity and quality of outputs. It can also lead to re-work, which cuts down on efficiency, drives costs up, and increases delays.

Needless to say, that makes controlling variation a critical part of process improvement efforts. Here are some terms you need to know before you learn how to make that happen:

Variation is divided into two categories: normal and abnormal. Normal variation describes the routine fluctuation of performance that you see in a piece of equipment or in the time it takes to get something done. Normal variation is predictable and usually occurs as a result of certain so-called common causes, such as the reliability of equipment or how familiar employees are with the process-related tasks.

Abnormal variation, on the other hand, occurs when the average performance of that same piece of equipment changes sharply in some way. Unlike normal variation, you can't predict this kind of activity, because it is due to special causes (for instance, an earthquake that keeps people from coming to work). As the term implies, this type of variation generally doesn't happen very often.

As you can imagine, different types of variation call for very different kinds of corrective action. Consequently, you'll have to determine what kind and how much variation there is in a process before you begin improving it.

Analytical Tools

In leafing through this book, you've already seen that it will help you use a variety of devices to improve your organization's processes. These statistical and other analytical tools are included to aid you in understanding and correcting variation-related problems. They're also useful when you're trying to figure out how to complete other key tasks, such as finding the cause of a variety of problems and determining how well a process performs. These tools will be introduced as you need them to complete each part of the improvement process.

Teams

Up until now, this chapter has focused on the different concepts and instruments you'll be using as you go about improving processes. But, you may ask, "where does teamwork fit in?" or "how come a few of us can't get together informally and hash this stuff out over the next month or so?"

What's Different Under TQM?

From An Organization That...

- Has many different and often conflicting goals among its divisions and departments
- Punishes mistakes, hides or rationalizes problems
- Rewards the following of established policies
- Lets short-term problems drive and dominate work activity
- Relies on inspection to catch mistakes before the customer receives the product
- Gives management full authority for top-down decisions for change
- Tolerates turf battles as inevitable
- Makes decisions arbitrarily
- Has a negative or indifferent self-image

To One That...

- Has a common vision shared by everyone
- Openly discusses problems, sees defects as opportunities for improvement
- Rewards risk-taking and creative thinking
- Focuses on long-term continuous improvement
- Improves work processes to prevent mistakes from occurring.
- Trusts and empowers employees to contribute to decision-making
- Facilitates and rewards cross-functional cooperation
- Bases all decisions on objective data
- Feels like a winner, with achievements creating good morale

The answer is this: Real improvement requires extensive knowledge of the process you're getting ready to improve. It also requires knowledge of other functions or processes that either affect or are affected by that process. Generally, no one person or even several people has such knowledge readily available.

In fact, you can't improve a process without the cooperation of various people who have a wide range of skills and thinking styles. Just one or two people simply can't supply all that's needed. For example, people who are very creative don't always have strong analytical skills, and people who are bold and aggressive may not have the patience that's needed to get the job done. Teams are formed, then, so that you as a group can use your collective talents to make your process improvement efforts a success.

Putting It All Together: PDCA

Now, as you know, all of these notions aren't worth much unless there's a way to use them. The Plan-Do-Check-Act Cycle (PDCA) is that way. All organizations that practice TQM use some form of PDCA. The basic steps of the cycle are:

- *Plan* what you are going to do to improve a process.

- *Do* an experiment to test the solution.

- *Check* the results to make sure the solution worked.

- *Act* on the results by permanently installing the solution in the process.

If this looks familiar, it is — it's the scientific method everyone learned in high school. This time, however, you'll be applying it to how work gets done.

What many people are used to calling common sense involves decision-making based on the assumptions they make about a given situation. They think everyone knows what is going on and what the results of the actions will probably be.

In fact, most people assume their way past PDCA's four steps. They assume they know the expectations of customers, how a process is performing, the causes and solutions of problems, and that improvements will automatically result from the solutions they choose. Unfortunately, real improvement doesn't happen that way.

PDCA makes no such assumptions. In fact, from the very beginning, you'll be challenged to let go of some of the assumptions you may hold about the way your organization does — or should do — its business.

During the Plan phase of the PDCA Cycle, for example, your team will learn how to define the process you'll be working on in a whole new way. You'll learn how to collect the data you'll need to measure the performance of that process and how to display the data you've gathered. Finally, you'll learn ways to use that data to solve the problems that prevent your process from performing at its best.

Next, during a discussion of the Do phase of the PDCA Cycle, you'll discover what's involved once management accepts your analysis of the process and decides to implement your recommendations on a trial basis. A description of the Check phase of the PDCA Cycle will explain how you and other members of your organization can determine how well your improvement recommendations are working. Finally, you'll get a sense of what will happen when, during

PDCA challenges you to let go of some of the assumptions you may hold about the way your organization does — or should do — its business.

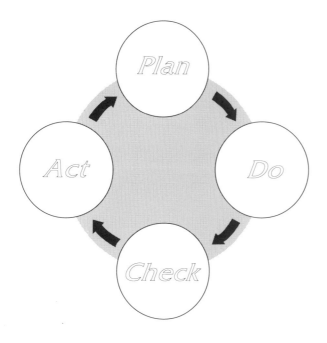

the Act phase of the improvement process, your organization decides to formally adopt the improvements you've made.

Congratulations on being chosen to participate in your organization's process improvement effort. The next chapter will give you an even better idea of what to expect.

The Plan-Do-Check-Act Cycle
A Framework for Improvement

Chapter 2

BECOMING A TEAM

As you walk into your first team meeting, you may or may not know many of your fellow team members. Chances are, however, that no matter how well all of you know one another initially, you'll probably begin your project functioning as a group of individuals rather than as a team. You'll also discover that your group's eventual success will depend very much on its ability to evolve into a team.

The difference between working as a group and working as a team is greater than you might think. Look at it this way: Could a group of NBA all-stars consistently beat the world champs? It's not likely. Why? Because basketball is a team sport and the difference between winning and losing generally comes down to teamwork. Members of a team must do more than shine as individuals. They sometimes must forgo individual preferences or star status, and assume roles that best support team goals. Sure, a group of all-star players might win against the world champs a time or two, but unless they practiced for months on end — in other words, unless they became the equivalent of a "real" team, themselves — they wouldn't stand a chance of regularly beating those world champions.

As you begin this process improvement effort, think of yourselves as a championship team in the making. You have the talent necessary to improve your process, and you'll be working together consistently over time. This book will provide you with a game plan that will see you through. Effective teamwork will give you the strength and stamina you'll need to emerge as both stars and champions.

In this chapter, you'll learn about team roles and why they're important. You'll also become familiar with the stages that teams typically go through during an improvement effort. You'll discover that decision-making in a team environment relies heavily on consensus, not individual leadership — something that's especially important to understand if you're a supervisor or manager used to making decisions on your own.

Finally, as you read this chapter, remember that there will be times when your team will be very productive and times when it will seem to be going nowhere. You'll probably walk out of some meetings feeling exhilarated and out of others feeling drained and frustrated. That's all part of being on a team, and knowing what to expect from the start will make the ups and downs you'll soon be experiencing easier to handle.

Building a Cohesive Team

To reach your improvement goals, you need to become a strong, cohesive team, but it takes work to transform a group into a team. Part of that work involves learning how to play various roles in your team, roles that will help to bring the members of your team together and accomplish your goals as effectively as possible.

Group Dynamics-Oriented Roles

Four roles are critical to team building: a coordinator, a networker, a harmonizer, and a gatekeeper. Team members usually share these roles. For example, during the time your team is working together, you may serve as a coordinator on one issue, helping to organize the project and get others involved. Yet, at another time, you may act as the team's harmonizer, keeping personal feelings from blocking team progress. These roles are described in greater detail below. Take the time to read them over and refer back to them as your group works to become a team.

The person who plays the *coordinator* role should be eager to build and achieve consensus on all the decisions the team makes. He or she should find it challenging to look for ways to use all the team's resources and match members' skills with the tasks the team must undertake to get the job done. Coordinators also help to organize and structure teams, make sure that all members participate in the team's work, and negotiate and resolve conflicts among team members.

Although your team would be hard pressed to use all of its resources unless someone plays a coordinating role, remember that no one assigned to this role will be successful if he or she overplays it. Coordinators who overplay their role may have the team spend so much time reaching consensus on everything that it never makes progress on anything. The best way to avoid such gridlock is to encourage consensus without losing sight of the team's ultimate process improvement goal.

Whoever plays the *networker* role will also see to it that every member participates in the improvement process. Networkers have to be especially sensitive to interactions between team members as well as responsible for keeping the team in contact with the rest of the organization. Networkers also keep track of other efforts in the organization that may work in concert with yours, and they discover who in the organization has the resources your team needs to complete its task.

Like all true networkers, the person who takes on this role will also make sure that team members and non-team members who can help each others' efforts are put in touch with one another — early and often. In this way, a successful networker will prevent the team from becoming isolated from other people and other ideas. However, networkers need to be cautious about making too many commitments to non-team members. It's important to seek cooperation from others without overwhelming the team with obligations that it may not be able to fulfill.

The *harmonizer* role is another that is vital to the team. Harmonizers quite literally help team members get along with each other and help them to explore their feelings about team activities. They also work to reduce team stress, promote respect for team members' different values and opinions, and emphasize the positive aspects of everything the team does.

Without a harmonizer, disagreements and other forms of interpersonal conflict may never be explored. If that happens, personal resentments and other unresolved feelings may eventually erupt into unproductive open conflict and make everyone miserable. On the other hand, if a harmonizer tries too hard to keep the peace, your team may avoid all conflict. This is a mistake. Constructive conflict can settle issues to everyone's satisfaction, but silence never can.

Another group dynamics-related role that one of your team members will perform is the *gatekeeper* role. Gatekeepers serve a parental or mentoring function; they make it possible for the team to achieve its goals according to previously agreed-upon rules. Gatekeepers encourage the team to stick to a code of conduct, point out violations of team norms, and make sure that all team members have an equal chance to take part in team activities.

Teams who decide that they don't need a gatekeeper may be in for a shock when no one is specifically monitoring the team's conduct. Without someone in the gatekeeper role, for example, team meetings may become frustrating free-for-alls.

It's quite possible, however, that other team members will see a gatekeeper as a nag if he or she is constantly critical. They could start to ignore everything a gatekeeper says, simply because he or she says it. To avoid such pitfalls, gatekeepers should be selective and constructive in their criticism of team efforts.

Getting the Job Done: Task Roles

As your team works through the improvement process, members may also play task-oriented roles: the shaper, the innovator, the analyzer, and the implementor.

Just as in fulfilling the group dynamics-oriented roles discussed above, team members may also perform different task-oriented roles at different stages in the improvement process. In fact, you may find that you play more than one role at the same time.

Shapers focus their efforts on helping the team begin its improvement effort. They work to set the team's overall direction, direct its goals, and set its priorities. As a team proceeds toward its goals, a shaper aids in keeping it focused on assigned tasks and tries to prevent it from wasting time on unessential work.

Without a shaper, some teams can flounder aimlessly, jeopardizing the effectiveness of their work. However, shapers who wind up dominating the team may stall its progress by pushing it to do things their way. As always, striking a balance between too much and too little control of the group process produces the best results.

Those who find themselves in *innovator* roles often serve as a team's "idea people." They can be counted on to come up with new ideas and offer a fresh perspective when the team reaches an impasse. In order to be effective, innovators must enjoy solving problems, help the team look toward the future, and encourage it to adopt new approaches to the way things get done.

What Makes an Effective Team?

In Effective Teams:

- Communication goes two ways
- Members openly and accurately express both their ideas and their feelings
- Team members share participation and leadership

- Decision-making procedures are appropriate for the situation — teams discuss issues and try to reach consensus on them

- Constructive controversy and conflict enhance the quality of decisions the team makes

- Members evaluate the effectiveness of the team and decide how to improve its work

In Ineffective Teams:

- Communication is one-way
- Members express their ideas, but keep their feelings to themselves
- Member participation is unequal: members who hold positions of authority tend to dominate

- Decisions are always made by members who possess the most authority – there is minimal team discussion

- Controversy and conflict are ignored or avoided, and the quality of decision making suffers
- The highest-ranking member of the team, or management itself, decides how to improve the team's effectiveness

---

When innovators are absent from the group process, teams may suffer from tunnel vision — they may not be able to look at a problem in more than one way or accept anything but well-worn solutions to complex problems. However, relentless innovators may hamper the team's effectiveness as well. They can inadvertently encourage team members to spend all of their time generating new ideas instead of devoting some time to implementing them.

Team members who play the *analyzer* role must stand ready to evaluate the new ideas that innovators and other team members present during the improvement process. Analyzers test these new ideas to make sure they're workable and point out unsound approaches to problems. They also insist that team members gather all the data they need to make informed decisions before they make them. Finally, they should like to break problems down into their component parts and rigorously analyze them.

Teams that don't have anyone playing the analyzer role and evaluating their work run the risk of developing flawed solutions and improvement plans. Remember, though, that if a team is led by an overanalyzer, it may get caught up in "paralysis by analysis" and never finish the work. The trick is to scrutinize ideas enough to determine whether they can work without alienating team members and bogging down the team's progress.

Those playing the *implementor* role, on the other hand, quite simply "make things happen." They keep the team on target, show team members how to get the job done, figure out what resources are needed, and help the team stick to its schedule and budget.

If a team does not have an implementor in its ranks, it may wind up by not putting any of its ideas into action, or it may not respect time and budget limitations. In short, it may miss some important deadlines and opportunities.

If the implementor role is overemphasized, however, trouble may follow. The team, for example, may overlook important aspects of a problem in its rush to finish on time and on budget. What's more, if implementors try to pin down resources too early in the planning process, the team may reject good ideas just because they can't immediately identify the resources needed to make them work. Successful implementors are generally flexible about ideas, deadlines, and budget considerations when they can be and tough about all of those things when they *must* be.

Which roles should you play? Read through these descriptions again, and ask yourself which ones seem most natural to you. Are you practical and goal-driven? If so, you may be a natural shaper. Would you rather come up with new ideas (be an innovator) or carefully test others' suggestions (be an analyzer)? Each role you play makes a key contribution to your team's success.

Other Roles and Responsibilities

In addition to the roles described above, all team members share a variety of responsibilities. These include:

- maintaining team momentum

- promoting quality improvement by publicizing the team's success

- setting an example for team behavior by their own actions

- getting help from those outside the team as needed

- keeping management aware of team progress

- contributing expertise to the team

- completing team-related assignments

There are, however, two other roles that warrant discussion: the roles of *team administrator* and *team facilitator*.

The nice thing about team-work is that you always have others on your side.

The *team administrator* performs several clerical tasks for the team. Such tasks may include planning and scheduling team meetings, taking notes during meetings, and maintaining a record of the team's work. While it's possible that one team member will take on this role indefinitely, it's more likely that team members will take turns serving in this capacity.

The *team facilitator* may be an actual team member, an organization employee who facilitates teams of all kinds on an ongoing basis, or a process improvement expert hired by your organization for the duration of your improvement effort.

Some facilitators, particularly those who are actual team members, will attend all team meetings. Others may participate on a periodic or on-call basis. In any case, they may be called upon to:

- serve as liaisons between the team and management

- act as technical advisors for the improvement process

- observe teams and mirror their activities

- instruct team members on how best to promote teamwork

While the facilitator must fully recognize that teams new to process improvement will need help, he or she must remain aware that the team can't get bogged down in the process itself. Otherwise, it won't grow into its responsibilities.

Decision-Making in a Team

The goal of any team should be to reach decisions that best reflect the thinking of all of its members. This is reaching consensus — making a decision that all members can live with, advocate, and implement.

When seeking consensus, your team must ask for and talk about the other side of every issue. You and your teammates must make sure the language and wording used to describe each issue is clear. Listen to others' ideas with an open mind, but feel free to express your reservations about any idea or approach your team might adopt.

True consensus requires a great deal of:

- thought

- trust

- time

- active participation of all group members

- creative thinking and open-mindedness

The next chapter contains several different tools you can use to further assist you in the decision-making process.

Avoiding Groupthink

The term "groupthink" is used to describe a situation in which an illusion of consensus rather than real consensus takes place. In such situations, team members accept ideas without scrutinizing their pros and cons or looking at alternatives. Considerable suppression of opposing opinions occurs. This can happen when:

- people are reluctant to upset what appears to be team consensus

- the team as a whole does not want to upset comfortable relationships that have developed among members

- someone in a position of authority pushes for a certain viewpoint

Helpful Hint:

Avoid "groupthink" while seeking consensus.

The symptoms of groupthink include:

- *The illusion of invulnerability and infallibility.* Things have been going so well that the group starts thinking they can't make a mistake.

- A *tendency to rationalize away data.* The group tunes out any information that doesn't mesh with any preconceived notions it may have.

- *Lack of questioning.* Members start to feel that the group's cause is so right that its methods should not be questioned.

- A *tendency to stereotype.* Group members insist that those who hold opposing views are weak, evil, stupid, incompetent, or "out to get us."

- *Self-censorship.* Members do not speak up because they fear what will happen if they disagree.

- *The illusion of unanimity.* Everyone pretends there is agreement, even though they know there really isn't.

- *"Mindguards."* People in the group take it on themselves to tell others what to think.

To prevent groupthink, your team must:

- encourage openness and expressions of doubt

- seek outsiders' reactions and opinions

- invite trusted outsiders to join group discussions

- assign someone the role of "devil's advocate"

- discourage opinions expressed by team members who enjoy higher status in the organization until others have had their say

DECISION-MAKING APPROACHES AT A GLANCE

Time Required	% of Group Involvement	Type of Decision	Description	Likelihood Of Action
NONE	0%	No decision	Issue is avoided– all members have directly or indirectly agreed not to discuss the issue	NONE
VERY LITTLE	20%	Decision by powerful minority	Decision is made by a powerful clique or individual– other opinions are not sought	VERY LITTLE
	40%	Bartering	Competing powerful individuals or cliques make trade-offs	
	50%	Consultive decision	Decision is made by a powerful clique or individual in consultation with "experts"	
SOME	60%	Majority vote	Minimal discussion of the minority point of view– the minority concedes "victory" to the majority	SOME
	80%	Majority rule	Decision by majority vote, but both majority and minority viewpoints are explored– majority position still "wins" and remains essentially unchanged	
A LOT	100%	Consensus	Needs and interests of all parties are explored and a creative and unified team solution emerges from considering all positions	A LOT

Making Every Meeting Count

Teams do most of their work in meetings. Since everyone has a permanent job to do in addition to their process improvement work, team meetings must be efficient. To keep your task moving, meetings must also be productive and creative.

Here are some guidelines to help your team get the most from its meetings:

1. Have an agenda for each meeting. The agenda should include the following information:

    *   agenda topics

    *   presenters of the topics

    *   time guidelines

    *   item types (whether the item requires discussion, a decision, or just an announcement)

2. Take minutes; have someone record the key subjects discussed, the main points raised, the decisions made, and the items your team has agreed to raise again. Rotate this duty among team members.

3. Draft an agenda for the next meeting before each meeting ends.

4. Evaluate the meeting by asking for feedback on how to improve the next meeting.

Completing Meeting Assignments on Time

At each meeting some team members will receive or volunteer for assignments for the next meeting. Team members, for example, may need to:

- gather data

- format data that someone else has gathered into charts for easy team review

- write up all the options the team will consider at the next meeting

You probably won't have an assignment for every meeting. When there are assignments but no one volunteers for them, the team's facilitator will give the task to the most qualified member. Don't worry too much about being swamped when this happens; he or she will "spread the burden" as fairly as possible.

When you do have an assignment, give it the same attention you'd give to a task in your regular job. Each assignment you complete helps your team move ahead — if you're late or unprepared, the process and everyone in it suffers.

Maintaining Commitment to the Team

Being a member of a process improvement team is an important commitment. Depending on the nature of your process, your team may be working together over a period lasting from several weeks to several months. During that time, you will need to balance your team responsibilities with your job responsibilities. If this becomes a problem, talk to your team leader or your organization's TQM coordinator. They can help you sort out priorities and work with your supervisor if time conflicts arise.

You will also need to balance your feelings about the team process with your commitment to a better work process. After all, no matter how well a team works together, every group will falter at one time or another. As your team moves forward, or backward, or sometimes not at all, so will the team mood.

Try not to take this to heart. As you read the next section, keep in mind that your team will probably go through all of the stages described there. The best way to deal with these developments is to

Commitment transforms a promise into a reality. It involves:

- making time when there is none

- coming through time after time.

remember that they're a natural part of the process. Adopt a "this too shall pass" attitude about frustrations. In process improvement, patience may be the greatest virtue of all.

Group Developmental Stages

Teams go through various developmental stages as they work together. Every team begins in the formation stage, then moves on to the conflict stage; both of these are foundation stages. During these foundation stages, roles become more defined. Conflict may also occur because different team members might not like what the group is going to do or what role they have. By contrast, the home base and synergy stages are called productive stages largely because the majority of each team's work gets done in these periods. Effective teams seem to spend most of their time in the home base stage.

You will be able to recognize these various group stages as your team progresses. Your team may very well move back and forth between these four stages, especially in the beginning. An understanding of them will help you to develop some perspective on your team's progress.

Stage 1 — Team Formation

All teams begin at this stage. During this time, team members generally feel excited and optimistic about the prospect of working together. They tend to act tentative and shy around other team members and, whether they say so or not, they also feel a bit anxious and skeptical about the task ahead.

At this stage, team members are primarily concerned with answering these questions:

- What is our team's purpose?

- What methods and procedures will we use?

- What will be acceptable team behavior?

- What will be expected of us?

- How will we be judged?

Stage 2 — Conflict

During this stage, team members are likely to argue about what actions the team should take and what methods should be used. In fact, they'll often resist collaborating with other team members.

As this stage progresses, team members will begin to feel varying degrees of concern about the team's chance for success. Individual members, and perhaps the team as a whole, will resist attempts to try different approaches to problems. An increase in tensions among team members and a sense of team disunity may prevail for a while. In fact, team members may feel downright defensive and competitive with one another.

By the end of this stage, team members may not yet be proceeding toward their goal, but they will have begun to understand one another. During this time, the team will be focusing on answering the following questions:

- How should conflict around the team's purpose and methods be resolved?

- How should the team deal with such problems?

- How will roles be decided?

Stage 3 — Home Base

During this stage, team members decide to accept team rules, team roles, and the strengths and idiosyncrasies of fellow members. By this time, the job the team has set out to do is getting done in a positive and effective way. Again, most productive teams spend most of their time in home base.

At this stage, team members are bound to feel a sense of personal accomplishment, belonging, and mutual trust. They also feel free to express ideas and to give and receive constructive criticism. In addition, it is now that teams generally exhibit a sense of unified purpose and a realistic awareness of the resources available to them. By this point, they have developed effective procedures for leading themselves, solving problems, and resolving conflict; they also display a good amount of productivity and honor their own team norms.

Stage 4 — Synergy

By this final stage, the team is an effective, cohesive unit that gets a lot of work done. While progressing through the synergy stage, team members feel creative, trust one another, and take pride in the team's accomplishments. Teams that have reached this stage effectively coordinate members' activities and abilities, make decisions by consensus, communicate well with people inside and outside the team, and are eager to participate in and volunteer for additional team activities.

Getting Started: Developing a Code of Conduct

One of the first actions your team can take to build a sense of commitment to each other and to your work is to develop a team code of conduct. Do this important job before launching into the task described in the next chapter, namely, defining the process you're going to improve.

Why? Because developing your team's code of conduct will determine, among other things, how your team will make decisions. Once that's settled, your task will become a little easier.

Developing a code of conduct will require you to examine the values, expectations, and habits you and others bring to the team. All of these things, in turn, will help shape the team's attitudes and behaviors, which are known as group or team norms.

Remember that there is not one "right" way for groups to behave — your team needs to discuss what will help you work together best. In identifying your team norms, you are developing a code of conduct. This code of conduct will indicate what type of behavior team members may or may not engage in while participating in the team.

As you establish your code of conduct, remember that effective group norms must be:

- understood and accepted by all team members

- helpful in accomplishing team goals and tasks

- created by the team, so that each member feels a sense of "ownership" of them

- enforced by all team members

- flexible — team members can set new ground rules if the original norms hinder the process

The following exercise is designed to guide you through the all-important task of developing your code of conduct. Take time to examine your potential team norms thoroughly — and remember, none are etched in stone. If necessary, you can revise them as your work progresses.

Group Developmental Stages

The Code of Conduct May Include:

- how to dress

- what words to use

- what "on time" means

- how decisions will be made

- what group roles are valued

- what behaviors to avoid

- what happens when you break the rules

Exercise: Creating Your Team's Code of Conduct

Task: To create a team code of conduct based on the task-oriented and people-oriented norms held by the team.

Procedure:

1. Brainstorm a list of norms that will affect how your team will operate.

2. Make sure that some of these norms are related to task work and some are related to group dynamics (people) work.

3. For each norm, identify what behavior you would be seeing and hearing if this norm were accepted by the team. Develop some hypothetical situations to see how it would work.

4. Check for consensus on the content and wording of your code of conduct. Can every team member agree to attempt to honor it as it stands?

5. Post your code of conduct in your team's meeting room.

6. Evaluate your team's process and allow time for feedback from your facilitator.

Once your team has comfortably established its code of conduct, you'll be ready to take the first step toward process improvement: defining your process. See the next chapter for details.

Chapter 3

DEFINE THE PROCESS

**The Process
Improvement Cycle**

Beginning Your Journey

Now that you have a
clearer idea of what a process
improvement team is and how
it's expected to operate, it's
time to begin the first phase of
your improvement effort:
defining your process.

Defining a process means
expanding a simple process —
such as requisition — into a
complete verbal picture that
identifies all of the key steps
and players in it. This phase of
the improvement effort is important. First, it gives all team members a common understanding of how your process actually works,
and second, it focuses the entire improvement effort.

As important as a common understanding of the process is, however, it does not always exist at the outset. Why? Because, for several reasons, team members may not view the process in the same
way. Some may be customers or suppliers of a process who bring a
unique but limited perspective to the team's effort. Furthermore,
when larger processes are involved, individual team members who
possess a detailed knowledge about a part of the process don't always
understand the big picture.

Defining the Process

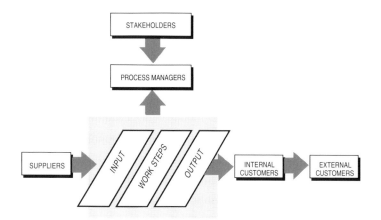

Key Actions

Collectively, however, your team should have the knowledge necessary to define the process. Your objective as a team will be to get everyone to contribute to the development of a thorough description of the process you've been assigned to improve.

Once all team members understand the parameters of the process, you can complete the remaining key actions:

- define the process

- evaluate the project plan

- develop the customer/manager interview plan

- conduct interviews

- prioritize expectations

Key Action 1: Define the Process

The first task facing your team is to draw a complete picture of your process. If your team received a formal charter from management, it may identify (from management's point of view) some of these process elements. It's a good idea, however, to put the charter aside until after the team has defined the process on its own. This will force the team to really think through this step instead of simply accepting management assumptions about the process.

To define the process, you need to clearly identify each of these process elements:

- process boundaries

- process flow

- process inputs and outputs

- process customers and managers

Process Boundaries

All processes — big or small, simple or complex — begin somewhere and end somewhere. These starting and end points form the boundaries of the process.

You must first decide when the process begins. Review the process your team is studying. Consider the people that perform the process work and where they fit into the organi-

Top-Down Flowchart: Process Improvement Method

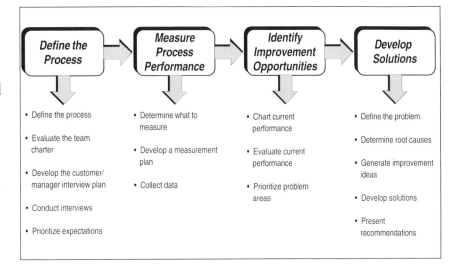

Define the Process	Measure Process Performance	Identify Improvement Opportunities	Develop Solutions
• Define the process	• Determine what to measure	• Chart current performance	• Define the problem
• Evaluate the team charter	• Develop a measurement plan	• Evaluate current performance	• Determine root causes
• Develop the customer/ manager interview plan	• Collect data	• Prioritize problem areas	• Generate improvement ideas
• Conduct interviews			• Develop solutions
• Prioritize expectations			• Present recommendations

zation. When do these people actually gain control of the process? If you can answer that question with a specific action, you will have identified the process starting point. For example, you may decide that your daily commuting process begins when you get out of bed.

The next step is to decide when the process ends. When do the results of your process get passed on to some other person, process, or work group? When do you hand over control? Answer these questions and you will have identified where the process ends. You may decide, for example, that your commuting process ends when you walk through the office door.

Process Flow

After you have determined where the process begins and ends, your next step is to identify what happens in between — what's commonly known as the process flow. At this point, your team should not be interested in analyzing the process, only in describing it. Don't worry about feedback loops, decision points, exceptions, etc. All you want to do is list the major steps in the order in which they occur. *The top-down flowchart of a proposal writing process (shown on page 32 in figure 3-1) is an example of one method that's used to capture a process flow.*

Figure 3-1

A Proposal Writing Process

Top-down flowcharts do not require that you list every minor activity that occurs in the process. Instead, focus on the major steps. There is no magic number of steps to shoot for, but each major step

should be able to be broken down into several smaller steps. The goal of a top-down flowchart is to graphically depict the process flow at two levels of detail, in sequential order. For further instructions on when and how to use a top-down flowchart, see pages 228-229 in the Toolbox of this book.

A *deployment chart* is another useful tool for graphically illustrating who does what and when. Like a top-down flowchart, a deployment chart illustrates the steps that occur in sequential order. A deployment chart can also show where each step is performed or who performs it — an individual, a position title, a work group, or even a function — depending on the size of the process.

When work flows out of and back into a process one or more times, a deployment chart can show clearly when and where these departures occur. This chart is also helpful when you want to illustrate the distance work must travel between steps. The example shown in figure 3-2 on page 33 shows a deployment chart for a requisition process. For more detailed instruction on how to use this tool, see pages 191-192 of the Toolbox.

Process Inputs and Outputs

All processes change (and add value to) something. Those things that get changed are known as process inputs. These inputs can be physical (for example, raw materials, parts requiring assembly, job applicants to be interviewed) or informational (for instance, instructions or computer printouts). Think of a document production process: Several inputs are possible, but the major one is an initial draft of the document.

Figure 3-2

Deployment Chart for Requisition Assignment Process

Process Steps	Clerk	Supervisor	Input Operator	Scheduler
Logindocument	X			
Sort	X			
Review for corrections		X		
Data entry			X	
Assignmentto purchasingteam				X
Review		X		
Distribution	X			

Your team needs to distinguish between process inputs and process components, which are the resources used to change the inputs. These components generally fall into the categories of people, materials, methods, equipment, and environment. Unlike process inputs, process components do not "come into" the process — they're a part of it. Some of the components of a document production process, for example, may be word processing operators, graphic artists, editors, computers, printers, software, binders, etc. Process components, in this case, are all the resources needed to turn a rough draft into a finished document.

The results of your process are known as outputs. Think of outputs as the products or services your process delivers to its customers. These outputs can be physical (for example, a finished, bound report) or informational (for example, a hiring decision).

Process Customers and Managers

A definition of your process is not complete until you have identified the customers and managers of your process. As noted in Chapter 1, all processes have customers, whether they are internal (within the organization) or external (outside the organization).

Process Components

A Process Consists Of:

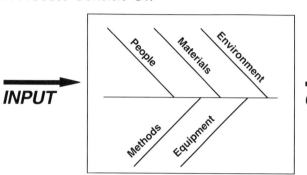 

Why identify customers? Because, as also noted earlier, processes exist to serve customers. Thus, customers must be involved in defining what a quality process means. Otherwise, you risk improving things that don't matter to the people you're attempting to serve.

If your process has many customers, it's a good idea to identify, where possible, the most important ones. You don't have to rank-order all customers, but if one or two are larger, more immediate, or otherwise more important, your team should acknowledge this. It may help you to distinguish between immediate customers (those who actually receive and use your outputs) and other stakeholders (anyone, such as a company president, who has an interest in or who is otherwise indirectly affected by your outputs).

You must also identify the people who manage your process. Processes can have one manager or several, each of whom may be responsible for part of the process you're working on.

Don't try to identify all of the managers or other stakeholders in your organization who might have an interest in or be affected by your process. While these people matter, teams should generally concentrate on the primary managers and customers of the process.

Key Action 2: Evaluate the Team Charter

Poor planning can waste time, frustrate team members, and even guarantee failure before a team ever gets started. So it's important that you take some time now to evaluate your improvement objectives. A little effort now can save a lot of trouble later.

Many teams receive a formal charter from higher management. Such charters usually outline the process boundaries, project goals, priorities, constraints, and other important elements of a project plan. If you have a charter, review it as a team. Be sure you understand and agree with its contents.

Some of the key planning issues for your team to consider are discussed below. It's a good idea to review these closely, even if your team has already been given a charter. Doing so will help you to determine if and where your charter may need a little fine tuning.

After describing the process, you should first determine if the process you are working on is an appropriate size. Management usually assumes the major responsibility for this decision, but improvement teams have the right and responsibility to influence it. After all, you are the ones who will study the process in detail.

Why is the scope of your process important? Target processes can be either too big or too small to make a successful improvement effort possible. If the process scope is too wide, the team will get bogged down. If the scope is too narrow, you probably won't be able to identify significant opportunities for improvement. Here are some guidelines to help you effectively assess the scope of your process:

- Review the major steps in your process flow. Are any of them subprocesses in their own right (each with its own inputs, activities, and outputs)? If your process steps are actually subprocesses, your scope may be too broad.

- Examine the height (the number of levels of authority) and width (the number of work groups involved) of your process to help assess its scope. Your process should involve relatively few levels of authority and only a few of your organization's work groups. However, this is not a hard and fast rule by any means: There may be times when more people can and should be included.

- Review the number of outputs for your process. There's no magic number here, but larger processes generally have more outputs than smaller ones. If your process, as currently defined, has numerous products or services, it may be too broad to tackle all at once.

Helpful Hint:

Here are some key questions to ask when you're assessing the scope of your process:

- Are the process steps we've identified actually subprocesses in their own right?

- How many work groups are involved?

- How many levels of authority are involved?

If your team feels strongly that the scope of your process is too broad, look again at the major steps. Sometimes, one of those steps may contain a process that's appropriate for one improvement team to handle.

Other Planning Issues

If your team determines that the process scope is reasonable, you're off to a good start. Here are a few additional issues to consider:

- Does the team include the right people? Collectively, team members should have a thorough knowledge of all aspects of the process.

- Are expectations clear? It helps to understand how you fit into the bigger picture. An understanding of expectations and priorities can provide focus for the team throughout the project.

- Are milestones clear and reasonable? Teams are often chartered to complete a process improvement effort by a specific date. Sometimes, interim milestones are established. These targets can help your team stay on track, provided that they're reasonable.

Of course, your task is always easiest when your team understands and feels comfortable with the project plan as presented in your charter. You should not, however, hesitate to seek clarification or even changes, if necessary. For example, if the team feels strongly that the scope is too broad or narrow, raise the issue with your manager or the individual responsible for chartering your team (generally referred to as a champion).

Similarly, if you feel key knowledge areas are not represented on the team, request that team membership be modified to address the problem. Sometimes, management expectations or priorities are not clearly stated. Get clarification if necessary. Are milestones unreasonable? Voice your concerns.

A good rapport between the team and its champion is essential and should be established right from the start. Everyone will benefit in the long run!

Keep interviews simple. Remember to focus on what your customer expects of your process.

Key Action 3: Develop the Customer/Manager Interview Plan

Successful process improvement focuses on customers. Whether your customers are internal or external, around the corner or across the country, your priorities must accurately reflect theirs. In order to determine what those priorities are, you must first ask:

How do customers measure performance?

This question is key because process improvement can't occur in a vacuum; you must first determine what customers and managers expect from your process. The next key action for the team, then, is to develop a plan for collecting information and opinions from important customers and managers. There are four elements to the interview plan:

- whom to talk to

- what to ask

- how to use interviews to collect the data

- how to assign interviews

Whom to Talk to

You must determine which people the team needs to interview to develop a sense of what customers expect from your process. Generally, teams should focus on their direct customers and process managers (managers who are directly responsible for your particular process), although external customers and managers should be interviewed as well.

Figure 3-3
Ranking Table

Customer Expectation	Importance	Current Performance
Cups don't leak	7	3
Cups are stackable for efficient packing and shipping	5	6
Cups hold hot beverages and don't burn hands	6	5
Cups are visually appealing	3	6

When the list of customers you could interview is large, it's not practical to talk with all of them. Fortunately, it's not necessary either. Pick a sample of customers. Identify key customers (biggest, most important, etc.) and include them. When appropriate, select a cross-section of customers to ensure that you've gathered a wide range of perspectives on your process.

What to Ask

Don't try to ask too much. Questions should be relatively few in number and open-ended. You can often learn all you need to know by finding answers to the following questions:

- *What does the customer expect?* You may think you know, but expectations are always changing. Focus customer responses on the outputs they receive from your process.

- *Which expectation is most important?* Customers will usually have more than one expectation. Your priorities should reflect customers' priorities.

- *How are we doing?* Customers may tell you that all of their expectations are equally important. Once you ask this question, however, they probably won't have any trouble distinguishing between the expectations you're satisfying and the ones you're not.

- *How do you measure our performance?* Offer examples of ways to measure it, such as how long it takes to receive a product. You'll quantify this later, but you can gain some useful insights during initial interviews.

- *In your opinion, what causes these problems?*

- *How could we improve the situation?*

Your interview plan can consist simply of the six questions above. You must decide whether asking more questions will work best for your team, but it's usually best to keep your interview simple.

Customers will generally have a lot to say about problems and their potential solutions. You may, however, have to urge them to talk about their expectations and priorities. If necessary, discuss the outputs they receive and get them to think of their expectations in terms of these outputs. Tell them that your goal is to focus the improvement effort on the one or two most critical expectations that direct customers, other stakeholders, and process managers have of these outputs.

To help you focus your interviews and accurately elicit customer feedback, you can use a table like the one shown on page 38 (figure 3-3). List all of the expectations identified by each interviewee, then ask each customer to rate both the relative importance of and current performance for each expectation on a scale of 1 to 7.

How to Use Interviews to Collect the Data

You can use a variety of approaches to gather feedback from customers and managers. Choose the interview strategy that works best for your team. Here are some tips to send you on your way:

- Face-to-face interviews are generally more effective than telephone interviews. A personal touch encourages people to open up, which, in turn, enables you to gather more useful information.

- One-on-one interviews are effective, but you can also work in teams or as a panel. If team members are uncomfortable conducting interviews alone, divide your team into small (for example, two-person) teams. It also may make sense to interview some key individuals (a high-level manager, for instance) using a panel format so that all team members can ask questions of that person and hear directly what he or she has to say.

- If possible, schedule interviews directly with the people you will be talking to, not their assistants. Provide a brief overview of the team's challenge, your progress to date (in other words, the efforts you have made to define your process), and the topics you wish to discuss. Use the outputs your customers receive to focus prospective interviewees on your process.

- Set an approximate time limit for the interview. Thirty minutes is usually long enough.

- Generally, it's a good idea to allow the interview subject to decide where to conduct the interview.

- Your organization's culture may dictate the need to "go through channels." Do bosses need to be advised of your objectives before you interview their employees? Take this into account when you set your schedule. Hint: Memos take time. Whenever possible, use the telephone. If you need help with logistics (such as introductions) from your champion or manager, don't hesitate to ask for it.

- Another purpose of interviews is to give people who will be affected by your team's recommendations the chance to be immediately involved. By drawing them into the process in a positive way, you will increase the likelihood that they will buy into your results.

Interview Guidelines

Be Prepared
- Organize your questions with your objectives in mind.
- Develop ways of asking for more information or following up.

Open the Interview
- Be relaxed.
- Try to build rapport by adapting your approach to the interviewee's style.
- Outline the purpose of the interview, indicate what types of questions you are going to ask and how you will report the data.
- Invite the interviewee to ask questions at any time during the interview.
- Explain that your analysis will be easier if you take notes. (If you want to tape the interview, first get permission from the person you're interviewing.)
- Make your first question open-ended — that is, not answerable with a "yes" or "no" — and easy to answer.

Conduct the Main Body of the Interview
- Probe when you need more information.
- Maintain control of the interview in a polite way.
- Watch the time. Don't take more time than you have scheduled.
- Stay attentive, listen carefully, and don't let note-taking get in the way of open conversation. If two team members conduct an interview, it's a good idea to have one take notes while the other talks.

Take Notes on "Body Language" and the "Feel" of the Interview
- Watch for physical signs, such as fidgeting or breaking eye contact, that indicate that a question makes the interviewee uncomfortable.
- Make a note if the interviewee accepts many phone calls or other interruptions, avoids certain subjects, or has a bias or attitude that affects his or her comments.

Closing the Interview
- Ask the customer or manager if he or she has other questions or comments.
- Let the interviewee know what to expect next, thank him or her, and leave.

Additional Suggestions
- Be genuine, sincere, and honest.
- Remember that the customer or manager is the expert on his or her needs.
- If you are asked questions that you cannot answer, make it a point to find out and get back to the person who asked them. His or her good will may be critical to the ultimate success of your recommendations for improvement.

How to Assign Interviews

The last step in constructing your interview plan is simply to divide the workload among team members. Some people will have preferences — whenever possible, it makes sense to accommodate them. It's also a good idea to keep a written record of interview assignments. You can use a simple grid like the one shown below (figure 3-4).

Figure 3-4
Interview Assignments

Team Member

Customer/Manager

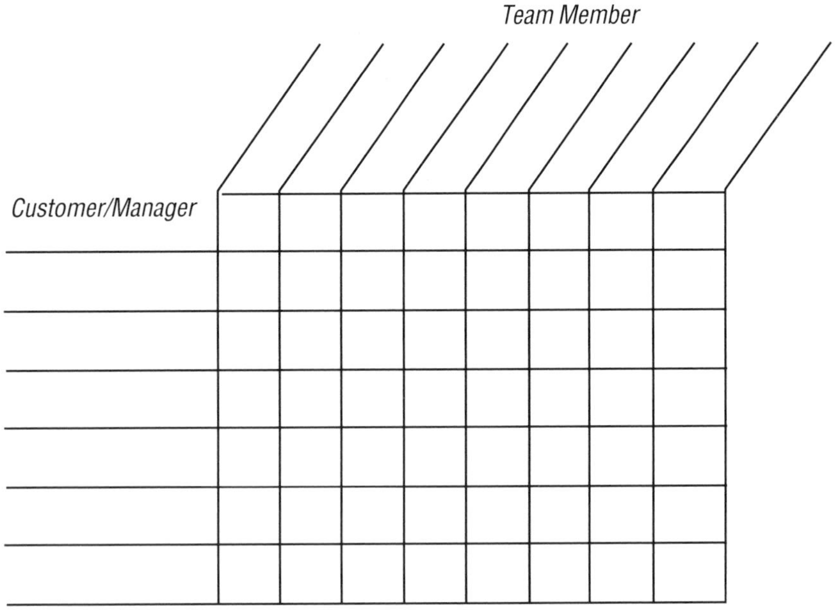

Key Action 4: Conduct Interviews

Once the interview plan is complete, the next step is to conduct the interviews. The interview guidelines on page 41 will help you structure your discussions and record results. In talking to people, be flexible. Even though you've got an interview plan, remember Murphy's Law — everything that could possibly go wrong *will* go wrong! Patience is always a good thing to take with you. Sometimes, interview subjects are cautious at the beginning, but experience has shown that, once they feel comfortable, they open up.

Key Action 5: Prioritize Expectations

After you complete the interviews, it's time to analyze the results and see what you've got. Remember, the primary objective of these interviews is to focus the improvement effort by clarifying key customer expectations. You'll probably also collect a lot of additional information that can be very useful to the team.

Summarize and discuss interview results as a team. List the expectations your customers and managers have. Make sure all team members understand each of these expectations.

Discuss customers' perceptions of your process's current performance. List and discuss both the problems they have identified and the improvement ideas they have offered to you. File them away for reference at a later date.

You can use the collective results of interviews, as well as any additional information available to the team, to develop an *opportunity grid* like the one shown in figure 3-5 on page 44. This is a simple two-by-two grid that can help focus improvement efforts by highlighting important customer expectations that are as yet unfulfilled. For instructions on how to use the opportunity grid, see pages 209-210 of the Toolbox.

The interview process often will make the most important of these expectations obvious to the team, but if you need more help in establishing priorities, try one of the following tools to define the process:

- *Multi-voting* will assist you in paring down the list of issues that your customers brought up during your interviews. A detailed description of how to use this technique is on page 206 of the Toolbox. The important thing to remember is that, in a matter of minutes, multi-voting can cut in half that overwhelming list of potential priorities you've collected.

And what if you've come up with so many potential priorities that one round of multi-voting scarcely seems to make a difference? The answer is simple: Take a few moments to conduct another round or two — you'll have a manageable list in no time.

- Using the *pairwise ranking matrix* requires more time and organization than multi-voting, but it's well worth it if your team needs to make decisions in a more formal way. This tool not only helps you to rank ideas in comparison with one another, but also requires a consensus-oriented discussion to determine which items can be paired and ranked against other ideas, according to your team's criteria. For a discussion of how and when to use this technique, see pages 211-212 of the Toolbox.

Figure 3-5
Opportunity Grid

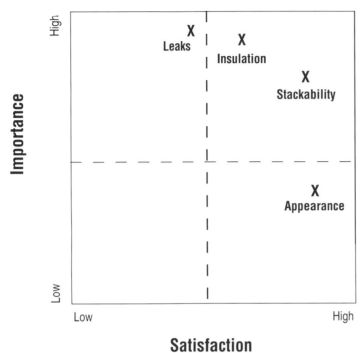

You are now ready to begin measuring your process performance. As you complete each of the successive steps in the improvement process, you will frequently refer back to the foundation established in this chapter. Each new step will add more clarity and focus to your improvement effort.

Chapter 4

MEASURE PROCESS PERFORMANCE

The Process Improvement Cycle

Preparing to Measure Your Process's Performance

In the previous chapter, you selected a customer expectation that will serve as the focus of your team's improvement efforts. That's a good start, but you don't yet have enough information to fully direct your work. Even though you may now know what results your customers expect, you probably don't yet know how to achieve those results — or even where to look for opportunities to do so.

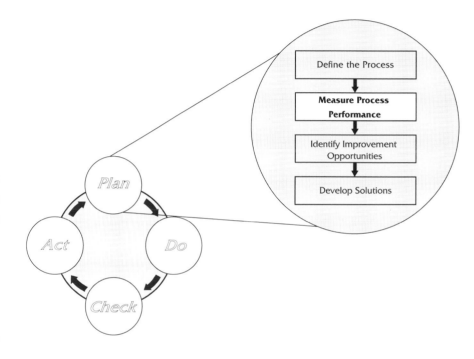

Your challenge, then, is to begin to establish a causal link between customer satisfaction and the specific actions you can take to improve process performance. By defining your customer's expectations, you've already taken the first step toward that goal. In this chapter, your team will be involved in translating those expectations from the customer's language into a language that's relevant to your process. That translation won't stand a chance of being fully understood, however, unless you discover how your process is currently performing.

Now, you might ask, "If we already know what the customer expects, why should we be concerned with current performance?" Well, there are two reasons. First, an understanding of your process's performance will help focus your improvement efforts where they'll

---

Top-Down Flowchart: Process Improvement Method

do the most good. Second, it's important to determine current performance so you can evaluate the effects of changes once you've implemented them. Traditional problem-solving often fails to provide ways to objectively evaluate such results. The steps you take here, however, will enable you to do precisely that.

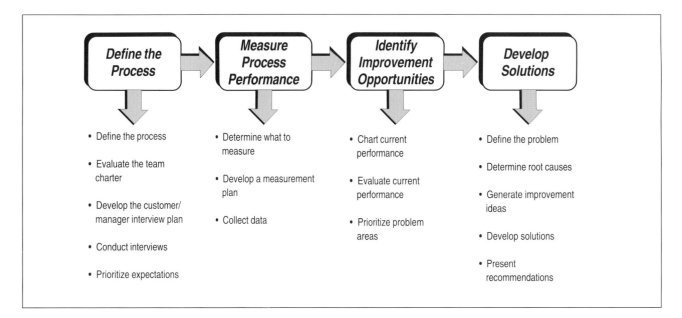

Define the Process	Measure Process Performance	Identify Improvement Opportunities	Develop Solutions
• Define the process	• Determine what to measure	• Chart current performance	• Define the problem
• Evaluate the team charter	• Develop a measurement plan	• Evaluate current performance	• Determine root causes
• Develop the customer/ manager interview plan	• Collect data	• Prioritize problem areas	• Generate improvement ideas
• Conduct interviews			• Develop solutions
• Prioritize expectations			• Present recommendations

As some teams begin their improvement efforts, they fail to see the need to rigorously measure process performance and collect the data necessary to do so. After all, they figure, team members already know the process and its problems well. So, all they need to do is fix the obvious problems, right?

Wrong. Such reactions are common but misguided. What you think you know about your process is often based on experience, perceptions, and intuition. But, as noted in Chapter I, such perceptions are often wrong, incomplete, or outdated. Effective data collection bases the decisions you make on facts — and a clear understanding of the facts is necessary for real process improvement.

Throughout this chapter, your team will learn how to take an objective, scientific view of the work process you've selected for improvement. To do so, you must determine what really drives performance. To succeed, you may also need to collect data that have never before been measured.

The rest of this chapter is designed to show you how to use key actions to measure the performance of your process. You will be asked to do the following:

- determine what to measure

- develop a measurement plan

- collect data

Key Action 1: Determine What to Measure

Once your team has gathered all the information it can on customer expectations, you may be tempted to tackle all, or at least most, of the problems that appear to be causing customer dissatisfaction. Don't give in to that temptation. Your team will ultimately succeed only if you solve the right problems — the problems that actually cause unsatisfactory performance and, in turn, customer dissatisfaction.

In order to find out which problems you need to solve, you must determine just what the cause-and-effect relationships between customer expectations and process performance really are. To do that, you must first ask a series of questions that will help you to determine what you need to measure. These are:

- How is your process currently performing?

- What are the output characteristics that are most related to current process performance?

- How can you measure performance for each output characteristic?

Answering these questions probably will not be easy; you will need to collect data to answer them. But as you do so, you will develop a thorough understanding of the relationship between what your customers expect and what you must do to meet those expectations. The rest of this section will show you how.

By examining the gap between what customers expect and what you're currently providing, you can determine how much your process must improve.

How Is Your Process Currently Performing?

Teams that begin an improvement effort with a broad, customer-focused problem such as "the process takes too long," soon run into trouble if they don't first determine just how long the process should take and how long it currently does take. Don't fall into that time-wasting trap! By talking to customers, you have already begun to clarify how customers measure performance and what level of performance they expect. But don't stop there — it is useful and perhaps even crucial to also document how your process is currently performing.

This gives you a performance baseline. By examining the gap between what the customers expect and what you're currently providing, you can gain a sense of how much improvement you must achieve to satisfy customers. This performance gap gives you a target to shoot for, and, if the gap's very large, it may alert your team to the need for major changes in your process.

Another advantage of documenting current performance is that it enables you to determine whether or not you measure performance in the same way that your customers do. When differences exist, as they sometimes do, your team can often gain important insights into what needs to be done during the early stages of your improvement effort.

Let's say, for example, that a team is chartered to reduce the time it takes for their organization to pay invoices. In their initial interviews with customers, team members find out that customers expect payment within 30 days. During data collection, the team determines that, while company policy requires that invoices be paid within 30 days, current performance averages 45 days. In fact, they soon discover that 25 percent of all the organization's invoices are late.

There's clearly a problem here, but a closer look reveals that there's more involved than meets the eye. Through customer interviews, the team found out the "delivery window" begins when the invoice is mailed and ends when it's paid. However, the team initially defined delivery performance from the time an invoice has been submitted to the processing branch until a check is written. The team did not measure the time consumed by internal and U.S. mail, although these factors clearly influenced customer satisfaction. In this example, differences between measurement assumptions might lead the team to one or more of the following conclusions:

- Current process performance is worse than initially expected.

- There are characteristics of total service delivery, such as postal service performance, that affect customer satisfaction but extend beyond the team's influence.

- The scope of the improvement efforts may need to be expanded to include internal mail operations or, if it's too large and its influence on delivery performance is significant, another team may need to be assigned to improve internal mail.

- Existing policy relating to payment of invoices may be insufficient to satisfy customer expectations.

As you can see, an understanding of current process performance provided this team with some useful insights that could very well influence the direction of improvement efforts. But the team must know more about their process's performance in order to improve it. Therefore, the next step must be to identify the characteristics of overall service delivery — also called *output characteristics* — that influence customer satisfaction. In order to do this, the team must ask this question:

What are the output characteristics that are most related to current process performance?

Answering this question is the first of several steps you must take to establish that cause-and-effect relationship between customer satisfaction and the actions your team can take to enhance it. Begin by reviewing the outputs you identified for your process. As you do so, you'll need to think about your outputs, not in abstract terms, but in the context of the specific customer expectation you're focusing on.

"In God we trust. All others must use data."

Dr. W. Edwards Deming

The following examples should help to set you on the right track:

The primary output of the invoice payment process referred to earlier is simply a *check*. The team's objective is not necessarily to change the characteristics of the check (the output) in some way, but to reduce the time it takes to deliver the check. In this case, then, the key output characteristics that the team needs to investigate should relate to the time involved in paying invoices, not to the check (the output) itself.

Therefore, the team needs to divide its organization's current invoice payment-related performance into each of its major time-consuming parts. For discussion purposes, let's say that the team went ahead and identified the following key output characteristics as major parts of the process:

- internal mail

- documenting for verification

- processing for payment

- approval and payment

- external mail

You may initially think it strange to include external mail as an output characteristic. Remember, though, it does consume time — and the time it takes to receive a check is one measurement the team's customers use to evaluate the invoice payment process's overall performance.

What's more, if team members discover that external mail exerts a significant influence on the time it takes to pay invoices, they might be able to do more than shrug their collective shoulders and conclude that that part of the process is beyond their control. In fact, the team could legitimately recommend that the organization explore other options, such as setting up an electronic funds transfer process, to speed the payment process and improve customer satisfaction.

Let's look at a different example, one that involves a product, not a service. Imagine a paper coffee cup, the kind used in vending machines. As a customer buying a cup of coffee, what expectations might you have about the coffee cup? Certainly, you wouldn't expect it to leak — and you'd also have the right to assume that the cup would hold hot coffee without burning your hand.

Well, that's what the customers of a paper cup manufacturer expected. Unfortunately, the company began hearing customers complain that their cups had been leaking lately. Distressed, company managers decided to charter a team to look into the problem.

How would they go about it? Well, let's try to examine the expectations described above from the improvement team's perspective. The output, in this case, is a coffee cup. The objective of the team is to identify characteristics of that cup that influence whether or not the cup is likely to leak. In all probability, the team studying this issue would identify the following two things as output characteristics of the cup:

- The coating is an output characteristic of the cup, since a thin, wax coating is usually added to the inside and the outside of paper coffee cups to prevent leaks.

- The glue is also an output characteristic of the cup, since glue is used to coat the seams of the cup to further prevent leaks.

As you can see, output characteristics will vary depending on the nature of the output — a product or a service — and the nature of the expectation. The key to successful process improvement is to identify output characteristics that, once measured, will enable you to:

- focus improvement efforts more clearly

- link the current performance of your process to problems your team can solve

The key to successful process improvement is to identify output characteristics that, once measured, will enable you to:

- *focus improvement efforts more clearly*

- *link the current performance of your process to problems your team can solve*

The key elements of a measurement plan include:

- what data to collect

- a plan for stratifying data

- a sampling plan

- what forms, check sheets, and data recording methods to use

- how to collect the data

The invoice payment team, for example, might transform its understanding of the problem identified from "it takes too long to pay invoices" to "invoice processing takes too long" or "payment approval delays are a problem." While the team's customers don't know or care about the approval process, if it takes too long, it represents a problem the team must solve to improve what the customer *does* care about — how long it takes to get paid!

Similarly, the team examining the coffee-cup leakage problem might transform their understanding of the problem from something as general as "too many cups leak" to something as specific as "the wax coating is not consistently applied with a uniform, specified thickness, which can lead to leakage."

In order to reach this level of clarity about the problem, your team must do more than just identify output characteristics. You must also measure the current performance of each of them. But first, you must ask the following question:

How can you measure performance for each output characteristic?

Your team must now agree on one or more measurements that will help you to determine the impact of each output characteristic on customer satisfaction. This is generally less difficult than it seems, but sometimes, when output performance is abstract or when you haven't measured an output characteristic before, your challenge will be a little more difficult. The following examples will show you why:

Our invoice payment team might decide that two measures are required to document the impact of internal mail on the time it takes to pay invoices. The team might need to determine how many days pass between the time the mailroom receives an invoice and the time the processing branch receives it. The team might also decide to measure how long (in days) it takes for a check to be postmarked after it has been written.

Whenever time is the characteristic being measured, it's generally easy to identify measurements you would like to use. Just be sure that the measurements you select accurately represent the time each output characteristic consumes.

It's conceivable, however, that you'll sometimes find yourself in situations where output characteristics are somewhat abstract and, therefore, not easily measured. For instance, a restaurant owner may identify "atmosphere" as a key output characteristic that influences customer satisfaction — but how do you measure atmosphere?

Well, perhaps the restaurateur could use such measurements as table spacing, lighting, and noise level to calculate the performance of his or her restaurant's atmosphere.

Regardless of the type of output characteristic you select, one rule holds: Try to use as few measurements as possible. If you can do the job with one, that's great. If it takes several, that's all right too, as long as each measurement supplies you with useful and necessary information.

If your team successfully answers the questions featured in this section, you'll have determined what to measure. Now, you must decide how to collect data. To do that, you'll need a measurement plan.

Key Action 2: Develop a Measurement Plan

A measurement plan answers the who, what, when, where, and how questions pertaining to data collection. What does that mean? Well, put yourself in the coffee-cup team's place for a moment, and think about how many questions may be involved. For example, it's one thing to know that your team needs to measure the thickness and uniformity of the wax coating on a paper coffee cup. But what tools will you need to do it? Do you need to measure the coating on the inside of the cup, the outside, or both? How many measures of each cup must you make to evaluate the wax coating's uniformity? Do you need to measure every coffee cup you make or can you measure a small sample of them? How can you make sure that the samples will accurately represent all the cups you don't measure?

You get the point. The list of potential questions goes on and on, and your team must decide which questions are important enough to answer and how to answer them. That's what developing a measurement plan is all about.

Keys to Successful Data Collection

Even the best-intentioned data collection efforts will fail if you choose not to heed some of the following keys to success. Keeping these in mind every step of the way will enhance your chances of success.

• *Be Patient.* Data collection is the grunt work of process improvement. Some teams are tempted to rush through this step to get to the more interesting work of problem-solving. Resist this temptation. Data collection provides the foundation for the work ahead.

• *Be Persistent.* With a little luck, your task will be easy. Often, though, teams are confronted with unfamiliar measurement challenges. Consequently, you don't always achieve the clarity and focus you need on the first try. If and when that happens, don't be afraid to change direction or try again.

• *Be Reasonable.* You want data collection to guide your actions, not bog you down. Don't try to measure too much. Manage the scope of your data collection efforts.

• *Be Disciplined.* Effective data collection requires some planning and, usually, some rigorous discipline — how much varies from one team to another. A good measurement plan can help you get it right the first time.

• *Be Resourceful.* Don't make it harder than it needs to be. Whenever possible, take advantage of opportunities to collect data that are easy to retrieve. Think ahead — if you do, you'll probably save yourself additional trips to files, computer records, microfilm records, etc.

The remainder of this section provides information and guidelines to help you. The material is organized around five major questions, which should include all of the major issues you may need to consider. However, your team probably will not need to address every issue in every situation. Use your judgment. Keep in mind that an effective measurement plan is clear, thorough, and as simple as possible. Be sure to develop a measurement plan that fits your situation.

As you develop a measurement plan, give full consideration to each of the questions. Remember that these questions should be answered for each measurement, and that the answers to them may change depending on the measurement you use.

- Which data will we collect?

- Which data subgroups will we look at?

- Which sample size, frequency, and sampling method will we use?

- Which forms, logs, or checksheets will we use to record the data?

- How will the measurement process work logistically?

The two categories of data are:

- *Performance Data,* which tell you how the process is currently performing

- *Cause Data,* which help you to determine why the process is performing the way it is

Which Data Will We Collect?

To answer this question, your team must make two basic decisions:

- Will we collect performance-related data or cause-related data?

- Will we collect existing data, new data, or both?

Performance Data Versus Cause Data

Performance data are, for the most part, descriptive in nature. They describe process results (your products or services) in terms of time, cost, quantity, and so on. Performance data tell you how the process is performing. Not surprisingly, you will rely primarily on performance data at this stage of the improvement effort.

To illustrate this point, let's return to the invoice payment process. As mentioned earlier in this chapter, the team determined that it took an average of 45 days to pay invoices. That's performance data. In this case, the team would also need to document current performance for each output characteristic — that is, the time required to move invoices through the mail, process them, and pay them.

Performance data helps your team to identify gaps that exist between what customers expect and what you deliver, and to locate problem areas and establish a baseline. Early in the effort, your team will collect performance data that describe current performance in "hard numbers." You will continue to collect performance data until after you have actually seen how the now-changed process performs. This will show you whether you've changed things for the better.

Cause data, on the other hand, focus on why the process performs as it does. Cause data support problem-solving by helping to isolate root causes of problems. For example, data that tell our coffee-cup team that leaks occur because glue is not applied in uniform thickness, creating weak spots, are cause data.

Don't assume, however, that you shouldn't gather cause data and performance data at the same time. Remember, resourcefulness is one of the keys to effective data collection. Sometimes, you'll know enough about potential causes to measure performance and isolate causes at the same time. The invoice payment team, for example, may measure the time required to process invoices (performance data) and simultaneously identify how many line items each invoice contains and which documentation, if any, is missing (cause data).

Most of the time, however, you won't know enough about potential causes until you've determined your process's current performance level. Bear this in mind: It's simply not more efficient to collect performance and cause data at the same time. Be prepared to document current performance first, then brainstorm potential causes and collect additional data related to those causes at a later date.

Variation: An Important Aspect of Performance Data

If someone were to ask you about your commute to work, you might reply that it takes 20 minutes. It goes without saying that your trip probably doesn't take exactly 20 minutes every day. In reality, there is some variation in the length of time it takes. On some days, you may arrive in as few as 15 minutes, while on others, the trip may take 25 minutes. Subconsciously, however, you select a value that lies near the midpoint of this expected degree of variation when you say "it takes 20 minutes."

If you collected data on your commute for a month and plotted them, you might get a picture that looks like figure 4-1 on this page. This picture — a *frequency distribution* — visually represents the variation in your commuting time. As you learn more about variation, you'll find that it's also useful to be able to represent such frequency distributions numerically. A couple of easy statistical values, such as the ones described below, will come in handy as you measure the performance of your process.

Figure 4-1
Frequency Distribution

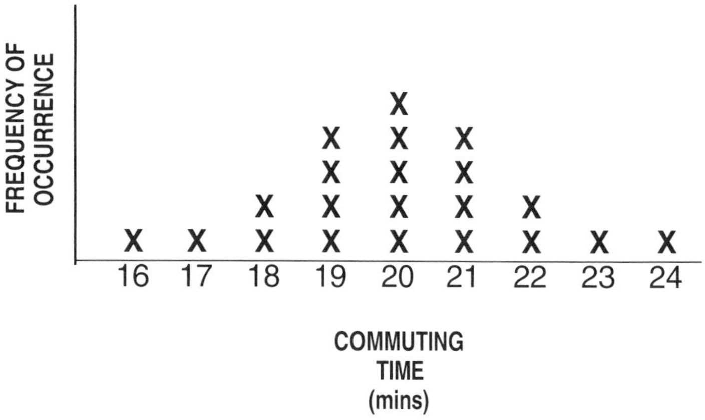

The average and the range are two basic statistical values that are useful for describing variations in performance data. The average, also known as the arithmetic mean, is simply the sum of all the values you've gathered divided by the total number of values you have. In normal circumstances, which will be discussed more in the next chapter, the average represents the most frequently occurring value; the rest of the data tend to bunch around the average. The range is a measure of the total amount of variation in the data you've gathered. It is computed by subtracting the smallest value from the largest value.

So, a more precise description of your commuting time would be "It takes an average of 20 minutes, plus or minus 8 minutes."

Why is Variation Important?

Recall that one of the uses of your data will be to assess the current performance of your process relative to your customers' expectations. Most administrative and manufacturing processes exhibit variation like that in the commuting process described above. And, as the next chapter reveals, this variation contributes to unpredictability, poor quality, and low productivity. Because of their direct effect on quality and performance, measures of variation that use average and range figures are easy and useful types of performance data.

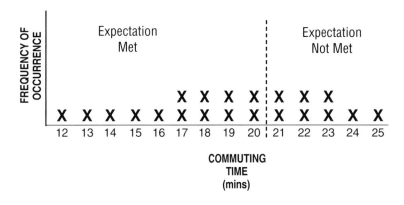

Figure 4-2
**Inspection-Based
Performance
Measurement**

It may be tempting to employ a more direct approach to collecting performance data by simply counting how often an expectation is either met or not met. For example, if your expectation was to make it to work in 20 minutes or less, a direct measure of performance shown on this page (figure 4-2) would tell you that you didn't meet this expectation eight times, or about 38 percent of the time.

This approach to measuring performance stems from the old "inspection" mentality. Traditionally, an inspector simply separates the bad from the good and records the number that are bad. These data may tell you that expectations are not being met and something should be done about it, but they provide little guidance as to what that action should be. It's more useful to collect frequency distribution data, which can help you identify root causes of variation and poor performance.

Existing Data Versus New Data

With any luck, data that relate to some or all of your measurements will already exist in the day-to-day records that your organization currently keeps. Investigate existing computer data bases, production reports, and quality assurance reports for information about your measurements. These records could contain much of the information you need to document current performance.

Later on, you can also use existing data to shed light on some of the causes of poor performance. Having existing data available makes the whole business of measuring process performance a lot easier, so use existing data whenever possible.

Remember, however, that you will often be looking at the process in a way that it has never been examined before. Perhaps no one has ever collected information that relates to some or all of the measurements you have selected. If that's the case, you'll be collecting new data right from the start.

Collecting new data is almost always more difficult and time-consuming than examining what's already there. If existing records, for example, had shown the invoice payment team the time associated with each output characteristic, the team could have quickly documented current performance at that level of detail. If, however, the records didn't include the necessary data, the team would have had to design a measurement system, track future invoices through the payment process, and record the necessary data.

Obviously, then, existing data is better than new data when it's accurate, relevant, and complete. Sometimes, however, when records are not designed to capture the information the team needs, there are holes or inconsistencies in the data. Don't use unreliable or questionable data just to save time — you'll pay dearly, later, for taking that shortcut.

When collecting new data, plan carefully and make sure everyone knows when, how, and what data will be collected. When team members are unfamiliar with selected measures, errors or misunderstandings are more likely to occur. Taking a little extra care is always a good idea.

When you *stratify* data, you are dividing data into subgroups or *strata* for the purpose of distinguishing between the different sources of variation in your process.

Which Data Subgroups Will We Use?

When planning your data collection, think of all of the information you may need about a measurement. For example, let's say your measurement of commuting time is the time it takes to get to work, door to door. Let's also assume that in your daily commute, you take one of two different routes, each about half the time. In looking for ways to improve your commuting time, it may be useful to know which points in the frequency distribution are associated with the different routes.

Figure 4-3

Stratified Frequency Distribution

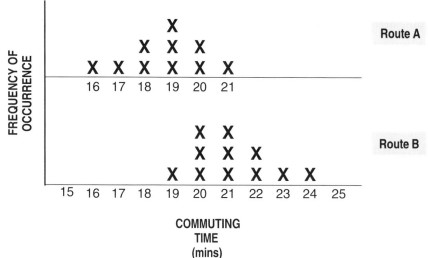

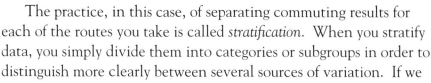

The practice, in this case, of separating commuting results for each of the routes you take is called *stratification*. When you stratify data, you simply divide them into categories or subgroups in order to distinguish more clearly between several sources of variation. If we had collected only one set of commuting time-related results without distinguishing between how long it took to take one route or the other, it would not be possible to determine if one route was consistently faster or slower than the other.

If you plotted separate frequency distributions for each route, they might look like the figure shown on this page (figure 4-3). Separating commuting times by route immediately shows you how to cut down on the time it takes to get to work: use only route A.

Time

For process improvement efforts, you will most often stratify your data into three types of subgroups: time, process components, and causes.

Almost always, you will find yourself stratifying data by time, if for no other reason than to discover how well the process performs both before and after improvements are made. Time plays an important role in most processes. Teams can frequently discover patterns and trends in time-related data that will provide important insight into what causes the process to perform at its current level.

Once again, the coffee-cup team can illustrate this point. Let's suppose, for the sake of argument, that this team discovered that glue application machines were adjusted every 60 days. Let's also assume that it found out that uniformity was consistent with the company's specifications, except for the last 10 days during that 60-day cycle.

Such a discovery might cause the team to examine the company's machine adjustment schedules. Perhaps adjustments are needed more frequently than previously believed.

In any event, your team should always note the time and date of the measurements it takes; it should also distinguish between hours, days, shifts, weeks, or whatever is appropriate for the process. If you were collecting commuting time-related data, for example, you might collect data on morning commutes versus evening commutes; how long it takes on different days of the week; or how long it takes during different seasons of the year. Once again, stratifying by time can often help you understand what causes your process to perform at a certain level.

Process Components

You can also stratify data by dividing the process into measurable components. For example, suppose you are measuring results that were produced using two or more machines, operators, or methods. Stratifying your process by each of these components could tell you if one machine was more efficient than the other or whether one operator is faster than another. This information could help you explain current performance levels and even identify improvement opportunities.

Our example of two commuting routes demonstrates stratification by process components. The routes can be likened to different methods or procedures in your process, which may contribute differently to the results you measure. Furthermore, what if the coffee cup process described above involved two separate machines that applied the wax coating to cups? Would it be more useful to learn, based on the data we collected, that the wax coating was not applied evenly or, alternatively, that a specific machine did not apply the wax coating evenly? As you can see, effective stratification by process component can give you better, more useful information.

For process improvement efforts, you will most often stratify your data into three types of subgroups:

- Time

- Process Components

- Causes

Causes

The third way you can stratify data is by causes of current process performance. As mentioned above, when your team has sufficient knowledge about potential causes, you can design your measurement plan to collect performance data and cause data at the same time. The invoice payment team, for example, might be able to measure the percentage of invoices requiring more than three days to process while stratifying these data by such causes for delay as errors discovered in the amount invoiced and a discrepancy in vendor records.

The commuting example can further illustrate this point. Had you chosen commuting delay times as your measurement, you could have stratified the data by distinguishing between such different causes of delays as accidents, construction, signal malfunctions, or bad weather. That's smart data collection. Of course, you wouldn't have used these data to study problems at this stage of the improvement process, but when the time came, you would have had the data needed to further examine the process.

What Sample Size, Frequency, Sampling Method Will We Use?

Sampling is a statistical tool that may make your team's job easier. If, for example, your process produces thousands of coffee cups each day, do you need to measure every cup to know how the process is doing? Thanks to sampling, the answer is no. Otherwise, the team would do nothing from now on but collect data.

Fortunately, the theory of *statistical inference* tells us that we can reliably view an entire process by measuring a representative sample of information. For example, you can measure total variation in a process just by measuring the average and range of selected information samples. You may be surprised by how small a sample you need to tell you all you need to know — but conducting an accurate analysis of your process depends on picking your sample correctly.

The Sampling Table

In order to pick samples correctly, you need to know how many items to measure, how often to measure them, and how to select each sample. The sampling table shown here (figure 4-4) will help your team make these decisions. To use the table, you first need to know:

Figure 4-4
Sampling Table

- the process rate (items produced per hour)

- the condition of the process

Process Rate (items/hr.)		Erratic	Stable
Sample Frequency:	Under 10	8 hours	8 hours
	10-19	4 hours	8 hours
	20-49	2 hours	4 hours
	50-100	1 hour	2 hours
	Over 100	1/2 hour	1 hour
Sample Size:		5-10	4-6
Sample Method:		Random	Consecutive or Random

The *process rate* is simply a measure of how repetitive the process is, and can usually be determined by existing data. Does your process produce 500 paper coffee cups a day or 5,000?

The *process condition*, on the other hand, relies on a judgment made by the team. Is the process erratic, or is it stable? This judgment is normally based on past experience, not on data. If you are unsure of whether your process is erratic or stable, it is always safe to call it erratic.

The sampling table is very easy to use:

1. Categorize the process as erratic or stable.

2. Enter the table at the appropriate hourly process rate.

3. Move over to the selected process condition column ("erratic" or "stable"), and read the sample frequency.

4. Move down the column and read the sample size.

5. Move farther down the column and read the sampling method.

Helpful Hint:

Many of today's pocket calculators have a random number function that can be used to select sample items.

Here's an example to illustrate how the sampling table works. Assume that the invoice payment process this chapter discusses pays about 200 invoices each week. Since the team finds a large number of errors and misfiled purchase orders, it determines that the process is erratic. The team establishes a process rate per hour of five by simply dividing 200 (the number of invoices processed in a week) by 40 (the number of hours in a work week). Looking down the "Erratic" column, the team then chooses a sample frequency of four hours, a sample size of five to 10, and a random sample method.

In an erratic process, there is a significant amount of variation within the sample period as well as between sample periods. Selecting items at *random* from all those produced during the sample period is the most impartial and accurate way to capture both types of variation. The invoice processing team, for example, would select sample invoices at random from the total week's output rather than collecting 10 sample invoices in a row.

What Forms, Logs, or Checksheets Will We Use to Record the Data?

Checksheets are nothing more than recording sheets that make data collection and analysis easy. If a checksheet is well designed, the data collector has little more to do than make checkmarks on the sheet to record data.

There is no specific format for checksheets; the format depends on the process and the type of data being collected. Page 65 (figure 4-5) provides several examples. For more information, turn to pages 165-166 of the Toolbox.

How Will Data Collection Work Logistically?

Your team is almost ready to collect data. Here are a few remaining issues to consider that are simple but important:

- *Who will be responsible for gathering and formatting the data?* Data collection is a chore and should be shared by team members. Sometimes, however, issues such as knowledge, access, or availability influence decisions. Let's say, for example, that the coffee-cup team decides to measure wax-coating results from the second shift. Since one team member works on the second shift, she therefore becomes the logical candidate to collect these data.

- *When will data be collected?* Don't delay unnecessarily. It's easy to find reasons for why you can't collect data. Set schedules and stick to them. Remember, the team can go no further until adequate performance data have been collected.

- *How will the team collect it?* Are any special tools or equipment needed? In many white-collar processes, no special tools are required to collect measurements. In some cases, though, software programs are needed to format computer reports. Other examples of measurement tools include a thermometer for measuring water temperature, a stopwatch for measuring time, or a computer for accessing records.

Figure 4-5
Key Action Checksheets

PROCESS DISTRIBUTION CHECKSHEET

Incoming Material

Weight (lb.)

	.46	.47	.48	.49	.50	.51	.52	.53	.54	.55	.56	.57	.58	.59	.60	.61	.62
									II								
							III	JHT									
						JHT	IIII	JHT	JHT	III							
				III	IIII	JHT	JHT	JHT	JHT	JHT	JHT	III					
	II	III	JHT	JHT	JHT	JHT	JHT	JHT	JHT	JHT	JHT	JHT	JHT	III	I		
Totals	2	3	5	8	10	18	14	22	15	13	10	9	5	4	3	1	

ONE-FACTOR ATTRIBUTE CHECKSHEET

Process step   Receipt
Department   Supply

Defect	Number	Total
Incorrect	JHT JHT JHT III	18
Missing	JHT JHT JHT JHT JHT JHT I	31
Misfiled	JHT JHT JHT JHT	20
Misrouted	JHT JHT JHT JHT JHT JHT JHT II	37
Total		106

TWO-FACTOR ATTRIBUTE CHECKSHEET

Lot no.	1	2	3	4	5	Tot
Type Defect	JHT III	JHT	II	JHT	IIII	24
	JHT III		I		III	13
	IIII	IIII	I		IIII	13
	JHT III	IIII	I	IIII	III	20
	III	III		JHT IIII		15
Total	32	16	5	18	14	85

	week			
Wasteful Energy Habits	1	2	3	Total
Long showers	III	I	II	6
Lights left on	IIII	III	IIII	11
Windows left open	II	I		3
AC set below 72°	I	II	II	5
Door left open	JHT	JHT	III	13
Total	15	12	11	38

Key Action 3: Collect Data

Your team is now ready to collect data. If you have properly developed your operational definitions and measurement plan, data collection and data analysis should go smoothly. Here are a few tips to keep in mind as you collect data:

- Give clear instructions to all data collectors, especially if there are any who are not team members. Are they collecting old data, new data, or both? Be sure to specify what kinds of data they are expected to collect and how.

- Ensure that data collectors have all the measurement equipment, logs, forms, and checksheets necessary to carry out their tasks.

- Let data collectors know how to reach team members or the team facilitator in case they have any questions or run into problems.

- Keep a record of who agrees to do what by when. Responsibilities are sometimes taken more seriously when they're written down.

Test the Measurement Plan

Depending on the nature of the process, it can take weeks or even months to gather enough data to conduct performance or cause analysis. Don't wait until the end of your project to find out if your measurement plan is working. Get together after a few days or so to look at the data collected up to that point. Questions you should be asking each other at this point include:

- Do data collectors seem to understand instructions, and are they following them?

- Is there uniform interpretation of checksheet blocks among the data collectors?

- Is sampling being carried out correctly?

- Are there any indications that data collectors are reluctant to record the bad news as well as the good?

Don't forget to get feedback from the data collectors, too. After the initial data collection period, they may have some good ideas for simplifying the procedures or enhancing the measurement plan.

Once you have collected sufficient data, you will be able to chart and assess current process performance. The next chapter will explain how to use your data to develop pictures of the process that reveal how well it's currently performing.

Chapter 5

IDENTIFY IMPROVEMENT OPPORTUNITIES

The Process Improvement Cycle

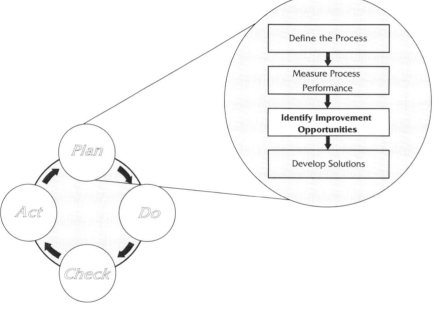

Charting Your Process's Performance

Now that you've collected some data, it's time to use it to determine just how well your process is performing. Then, once you've learned how to do that, you'll be ready to focus on what you need to do to improve process performance — and customer satisfaction.

As you'll soon see, a lot of statistical information will be presented in the upcoming pages. That's not a reason to skip ahead, however. Such information will be explained in straightforward language that's designed to take the mystery out of statistics. In addition, step-by-step instructions for using statistical tools are included in the Toolbox.

Familiarity with statistical formulas may not be necessary in your case — charting process performance can sometimes be very simple and require very little statistical analysis. To find out what's in store for your team, however, you must meet the first challenge outlined for you in this chapter — deciding which charting tools to use.

After that, you'll be asked to make the leap from analyzing the performance results your charts and graphs reveal to actual problem-solving. To do this, you must first identify the strengths and weaknesses in each key area of your process's performance. You can then study the process flow and go on to:

- develop a list of problems occurring in your process that may contribute to poor performance

- select the critical few problems that, if solved, offer the best opportunity to achieve improvement objectives

The remainder of this chapter provides information and guidelines to help you complete the following key actions:

- chart current performance

- evaluate current performance

- prioritize problems

Remember, charting and evaluating current performance can sometimes be very simple tasks. Because the range of charting options is broad, step-by-step guidelines for your particular process cannot be specifically provided to you. Instead, you must exercise judgment and select alternatives that best reflect your situation. You will need to complete each of the key actions listed here, but how you do so will vary from team to team.

Key Action 1: Chart Current Performance

Top-Down Flowchart: Process Improvement Method

This chapter presents seven charting tools designed to help you respond to a range of potential needs. Be sure to treat each measure separately when deciding which charting tools to use. You may, for example, decide that one measure requires a control chart, while the remaining measures can be displayed effectively using only a pie chart. The basic charting tools available to you are:

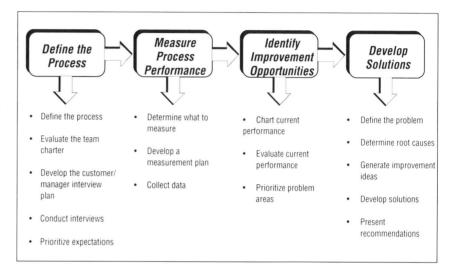

Define the Process	**Measure Process Performance**	**Identify Improvement Opportunities**	**Develop Solutions**
• Define the process	• Determine what to measure	• Chart current performance	• Define the problem
• Evaluate the team charter	• Develop a measurement plan	• Evaluate current performance	• Determine root causes
• Develop the customer/ manager interview plan	• Collect data	• Prioritize problem areas	• Generate improvement ideas
• Conduct interviews			• Develop solutions
• Prioritize expectations			• Present recommendations

- bar charts

- pie charts

- tables

- histograms

- run charts

- control charts

- pareto diagrams

Selecting the Right Tools

Bar charts, pie charts, and tables are the most basic charting tools. They are particularly effective when you need only to display performance data. They present data in a manner that is easy on the eye and easy to interpret.

These tools should be used when you want to display attribute data (such as the percentage of defective goods) selected from a specific period of time (for instance, a week, a month, a quarter, etc.). Don't use them when you need to evaluate trends over a period of time or when variation is an important issue.

Instructions on how and when to use the tools mentioned below are in the Toolbox.

Bar charts. This easy-to-make, easy-to-read tool very clearly shows quantities and the relationships between them. You might use a simple bar chart to display a simple measure, such as a breakdown of employees by years of service, as shown on page 73 (figure 5-1).

Pie charts. This tool is generally used to display the division of a whole into its various parts. It is especially useful in displaying proportions when there are not too many categories to consider, as seen in figure 5-2 on page 74.

Tables. Tables organize data into an easy-to-read format. There are many ways of presenting data in tabular form; the example below illustrates the breakdown of employees by gender for each labor category.

Labor Category	Male	Female
Manager	73%	27%
Production	68%	32%
Technical	50%	50%
Clerical	20%	80%

Using Charting Tools to Analyze Variation

It's important not to make your task more difficult than it has to be, so, by all means, use simple, presentation-oriented charting tools like the ones above whenever they're all you need to get the job done. Often, however, teams need to evaluate as well as display the data they've collected in order to understand how processes are performing.

The task of evaluating data often requires you to study the role of variation in your process. Why? Because the presence of variation in a process generally prevents you from clearly understanding what's going on, right away.

When this happens, you can use a histogram, run chart, control chart, or perhaps all three, to help you interpret your data. These tools, like the diagnostic machines and tests that doctors rely on every day, provide you with pictures that allow you to see things that you couldn't see otherwise. In short, they make your data more meaningful in many ways.

In the previous chapter, we mentioned that the variation that exists in a process may not show up the first time you measure process performance. In fact, you'll probably need to look at your performance data from several perspectives before you discover where and what type of variation is occurring. Some examples of the kinds of questions you may soon be asking and the tools you can use to get those questions answered are:

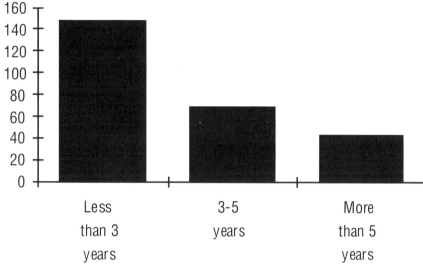

Figure 5-1
Employees by Years of Service

- What is the total variation in the process? Histograms will help you here.

- What is the long-term predictability of the process? Run charts and control charts will provide the answer.

- What is the short-term stability of the process? Control charts (of range values) will reveal this.

- Is the variation normal or abnormal? All three charts can help distinguish between these two types of variation.

As you read on, you'll learn more about these different perspectives on variation. This chapter will describe how and when to use histograms, run charts, and control charts. To help you understand how these tools work, you'll also be introduced to a few statistical concepts that involve normal and abnormal variation, normal and abnormal distributions, standard deviation, and in-control versus out-of-control processes.

Figure 5-2
Revenues by Product Line

These concepts aren't as tough as they sound. With a minimum of effort, you'll be able to learn all you need to know to use these charting tools effectively. Let's begin with a closer look at the issue of variation.

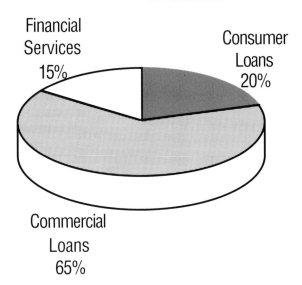

Financial Services 15%

Consumer Loans 20%

Commercial Loans 65%

Understanding Variation

At this point, you may be wondering why this book emphasizes variation as much as it does. Well, the truth of the matter is, variation is frequently the cause of unsatisfactory performance in government and industry today. It is often the source of unnecessary job-related problems; even small amounts of it, when present in dozens of interrelated subprocesses, can have a tremendous cumulative effect. Here are just some of the effects variation can produce:

- unpredictable performance

- additional reviews and inspections

- undesirable results

- avoidable rework and/or scrap

- schedule delays

- lower productivity

- lower reliability

- higher costs

- customer dissatisfaction (which, by definition, means poor quality)

Without an understanding of variation and its consequences, many organizations simply accept reviews, rework, and long delivery times as the price of doing business. Even when they do try to improve things, organizations generally look in all the wrong places — because variation masks the link between an effect and its causes. Once you understand variation, you can improve quality, increase productivity, and reduce costs all at the same time — by relying on a single set of consistent activities that continuously reduce process variation.

It's important to understand the difference between *normal* and *abnormal* variation.

Normal vs. Abnormal Variation

To deal effectively with variation in your process, it's important for you to understand the difference between the two basic types of variation — normal and abnormal. All processes possess normal variation to some degree, but the amount of normal variation they possess is crucial, because it reflects the extent of the problems and inefficiencies that exist in a process.

Processes can contain what's known as abnormal variation as well. Unlike normal variation, however, abnormal variation is caused by factors that exist outside of a process. That's significant. Why? The answer is simple. If your process does not cause this kind of variation, then changing it won't help you to eliminate your problems.

The importance of this distinction might not seem obvious at first, but what it all boils down to is this: The difference between normal and abnormal variation isn't immediately apparent to the naked eye.

That's where tools come in handy. Statistical tools such as histograms, run charts, and control charts can help you to distinguish between normal and abnormal variation. They can also help you to avoid:

- overestimating the impact of process problems

- making changes that aren't necessary or that won't work

To illustrate this further, let's return to the commuting example discussed in Chapter IV. What may have caused your commuting time to be different today from what it was yesterday? Your list of causes may include such things as variation in traffic patterns, the way that you hit the traffic lights, and the time that you left your house. It may also include your car's engine trouble, the flat tire you had, or accidents that took place along the way.

Although all of the above contributed to variation in your commuting time, you would probably put the first set of causes in a different category from the second set. What is it that makes the two different?

Variation in traffic patterns, traffic-light sequence, and departure time are:

- Fundamental components of the commuting process — you experience these common causes of variation in commuting time every day.

- Predictable — although it is impossible to predict how long your commute will take tomorrow, you can predict that these sources of variation will be present and so the resulting commuting time will fall within certain limits.

- Improvable — you can improve the situation by making fundamental changes to components of the process, such as selecting a new route or a different time of day to commute.

These are, therefore, among the causes of *normal* variation.

Flat tires, accidents, and engine trouble, on the other hand, are:

- Due to unusual causes — they can occur during your commute but are not considered a normal part of the process.

- Unpredictable — you can't really predict when you'll have engine trouble or a flat tire, or what the precise impact will be on your commuting time.

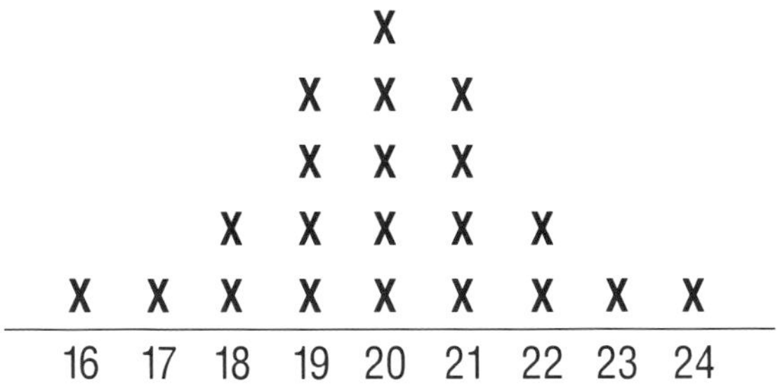

- Manageable — you can take certain preventive measures against such problems, such as maintaining your tires and engine or driving defensively. You might also minimize the effects of these unpredictable events by carrying a spare tire, jack, and set of tools in your car.

These are, therefore, some of the causes of *abnormal* variation.

This example should help you discern the difference between normal and abnormal variation, but it also demonstrates the importance of treating them differently. Imagine, for example, that one day a major accident turns your 20-minute commute into a two-hour nightmare. You wouldn't change your routine the next day — you'd probably see the accident for what it was — a special cause of delay. A histogram can help your team make similarly correct decisions about the variation in your process.

Using Histograms

A *histogram* is a bar graph that displays the results for a sample of performance data (daily commuting time, for example) in picture form. This picture is sometimes called a *frequency distribution* because it shows clearly how frequently each separate value appears in the data. You could display a frequency distribution using X's, like the example shown above (figure 5-3), but this approach is impractical when your sample includes a lot — perhaps hundreds — of individual measures.

In addition to being easy to use, histograms help to identify and explain variation in several ways. First, they clearly show the total amount of variation in the data, which is sometimes referred to as the spread. A bar at one end of the graph represents the lowest value in the data and a bar at the other end represents the highest values in the data. Together, they show the spread of the data.

Figure 5-3

Commuting Time for 1 Month (in minutes)

```
                    X
                X   X   X
                X   X   X
            X   X   X   X   X
    X   X   X   X   X   X   X   X   X
   ─────────────────────────────────────
   16  17  18  19  20  21  22  23  24
```

A histogram also reveals what's called the *central tendency* of the data. For example, the mode — the most frequently appearing value — shows one measure of that central tendency: It's readily apparent because it's the tallest bar in the graph. Another measure of central tendency is the average of the values contained in the data. When the data are normally distributed, the average value will equal the mode.

The most important insights about variation that can be gleaned from histograms are based on the shape of each graph. Once you understand how to interpret the shape of the graph, you can look at a histogram and generally tell not only how much variation is represented in the data, but also whether that variation is normal or abnormal. Before you can interpret the shape of a histogram, though, you'll need to know what normal and abnormal shapes (or distributions) actually look like.

Normal Distribution

A distribution can have an infinite number of possible shapes, but only a few occur naturally in processes, and one, the normal distribution, occurs more frequently than the others. A normal distribution has several unique characteristics that enable you recognize it easily:

- It resembles a bell-shaped curve — like the example shown on page 79 (figure 5-4). As you can see, the curve is formed by the frequency distribution of your sample data, which, in this case, are a sample of daily commuting times.

- The curve has a single "peak" or mode. In our example, the mode is 20, the value that appears in the data more frequently than any other.

- The mode is equal to the average of the data, which means that the peak is located in the center of the curve.

- The curve is more or less symmetrical on either side of the peak. In the example above, for instance, the values 19 and 21 each occur four times in the data, the values 18 and 22 each occur twice in the data, and so on.

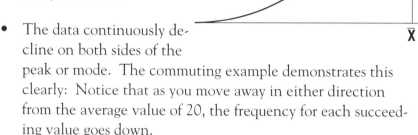

Figure 5-4

The Normal Distribution

single peak equal to average

symmetrical sides

continuously declining on both sides

X̄

- The data continuously de-cline on both sides of the peak or mode. The commuting example demonstrates this clearly: Notice that as you move away in either direction from the average value of 20, the frequency for each succeed-ing value goes down.

Abnormal Distributions

Your histogram can take on a number of shapes that do not re-semble a bell-shaped curve or display the other characteristics of nor-mal distribution. The specific appearance of these other shapes can help you to understand the variation in your data. In fact, these ab-normal distributions generally indicate the presence of abnormal variation.

Shapes A–E, shown on page 80 (figure 5-5), represent a variety of abnormal distributions. Here are some guidelines for interpreting what these shapes mean:

- Shape A contains some data that are isolated from the rest of the distribution. If you look at the bar graph (excluding for a moment the isolated bar), you can see that its shape resem-bles a normal curve. What's going on here? Well, it would be correct to conclude that the variation in your data is mostly normal (represented by the primary bar graph) but

Figure 5-5

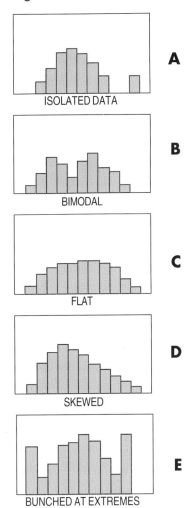

A
ISOLATED DATA

B
BIMODAL

C
FLAT

D
SKEWED

E
BUNCHED AT EXTREMES

Types of Abnormal Distributions

that it also contains some abnormal variation (represented by the isolated bar).

- Shape B is called a bimodal distribution because, as you can see, it has two peaks or modes. This distribution can occur when you fail to correctly stratify your data by, for example, grouping together data from two separate sources, such as machines, lots, and operators that have different performance characteristics. If you look closely, you can see that this shape actually resembles two normal curves side-by-side.

- Shape C is called a flat distribution because it doesn't have a single peak and it doesn't decline continuously as you move away from the center. This distribution could indicate that you failed to correctly stratify your sample, or it might signal the presence of excessive normal variation. If your histogram resembles this shape, you'll need to use a run chart and perhaps a control chart to understand the variation in your process clearly.

- Shape D is a skewed distribution because, while it does have a single peak and declines continuously on both sides of the peak, its shape is not symmetrical. This distribution usually indicates that abnormal variation is present, but on only one side of the mode. This distribution might occur, for example, if you were measuring variation in time at a point near zero, where values could vary freely on the plus side but could not dip below zero.

- Shape E is a bunched distribution because peaks occur at the center of and at one or both ends of the bar graph. These abnormal peaks generally indicate data recording errors. This distribution sometimes occurs when recorders "fudge" the numbers because they're afraid to record bad results — measures that are outside specifications, for example.

For further information on how to use a histogram, see pages 200-202 of the Toolbox.

Once you understand how to interpret the shape of a histogram,

your team can use this tool to learn a lot about variation in your process. But a histogram looks at variation in a fixed point in time — a
day, a week, or a month, for example. You can learn still more about

Figure 5-6
**Three Different Run
Charts with the
Same Distribution**

The commuting times shown
in this histogram could have
occurred in many different
sequences. Three possibilities appear below.

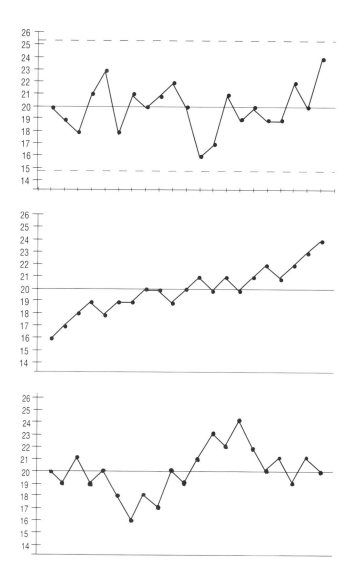

This chart shows what
might be expected from a
random process and dis-
plays no abnormalities.

This chart shows a rising
trend in commuting time.
This non-random characteristic represents a type of
abnormal variation. The
cause of this trend should
be investigated and action
should be taken to remove
the cause.

This chart shows a cyclical
or periodic tendency in the
data. Again, this is a non-
random pattern and is generally the result of an iden-
tifiable special cause.

Figure 5-7
Run Chart

variation by documenting its presence over an extended period of time. Run charts can do this for you.

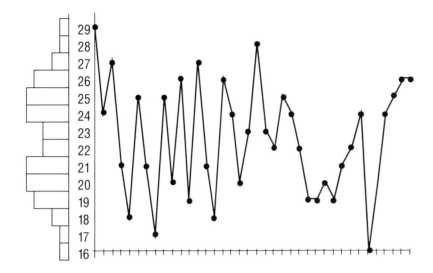

Using Run Charts

A *run chart* is a line graph that displays data measures in sequential order for such key performance issues as productivity, errors, or even the time involved in a process. By studying variation over time in your data, you can detect trends or cycles in your process. Both of these are examples of abnormal variation that would not be apparent using a histogram.

Because trends and cycles are indications of abnormal variation, you can usually locate one or two special causes for them. For example, a steady upward trend in your commuting time to work might be the result of increasing private and commercial development, which causes a fundamental change in the conditions that affect your commute — that is, abnormal variation.

To illustrate this further, look at the three run charts shown on page 81 (figure 5-6). Each contains the same 21 data points from the commuting-time histogram, but, as you can see, each run chart presents a very different picture of variation. The only difference between them is the order in which the individual measures are plotted. A run chart, therefore, can tell you things about variation that a histogram cannot.

The reverse is also true. Look at the run chart and its corresponding histogram shown on this page (figure 5-7). No trends or cycles are obvious from the run chart: The distribution of values appears to be random, which also is an indication of normal variation. Yet the histogram shows a different picture. You can see a bimodal distribution in the histogram — an indication of abnormal variation.

These examples demonstrate the value of using both histograms and run charts to analyze variation in your process, since one chart alone can sometimes present an incomplete, or even false, picture of process performance. For a more detailed discussion of how to use a run chart, turn to pages 221-222 of the Toolbox.

Figure 5-8

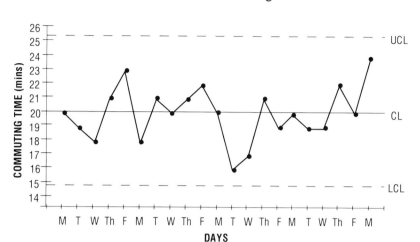

Control Chart

Using Control Charts

Like histograms and run charts, control charts are designed to help you study, analyze, and understand process performance. While histograms provide you with a kind of snapshot of a process and run charts allow you to identify trends in process performance, control charts combine the power of both of these charts to create a sort of *motion* picture of your process.

You can also count on control charts to tell you definitively whether or not the variation in your process is normal or abnormal. But they can do more than merely categorize variation: They can predict, within certain limits, how your process will perform in the future.

Like run charts, control charts require you to indicate the outcomes of a process in the order in which they occur. However, you need to add three simple but important lines to run charts to make them into control charts. These control lines define the boundaries of normal variation. Remember, there's nothing magic about arriving at these control limits. They're based on the past performance of your process and determined by using a few statistics — the average and the range for your sample data.

Control Lines

Now that you know that the data in your sample determine where your control lines are placed, take a moment to look at the three horizontal control lines that appear on page 83 (figure 5-8):

- The solid line in the middle is called a center line (CL). It represents the average of all the individual measures in your sample data. In a normal distribution, as you recall, the average represents the central tendency of the distribution.

- The broken lines at the top and bottom of the chart are known respectively as the upper control limit (UCL) and the lower control limit (LCL). These control lines tell you that given how your process has performed in the past (and assuming that the process is not fundamentally changed), you can expect to see future results fluctuate randomly between these particular limits.

Values that fall above or below these limits generally indicate the presence of abnormal variation. But keep this in mind: non-random distributions, such as trends or cycles, also indicate the presence of abnormal variation — even when all of the points fall within the control limits.

Remember also that control limits are not established on the basis of desired results; they don't necessarily reflect company specifications or policy. Instead, control limits are based on a statistical evaluation of the data and represent a distance of three standard deviations above or below the center line on the chart.

What's a standard deviation? It's a value, a measure of variability, that's derived by using a mathematical formula. It can be either large or small, and it can result in a little or a lot of variation in your process. Assume, for example, that the average of your sample data is eight and the standard deviation is one. Your control limits would be set at 11 and five — three standard deviations above and below the average or center line. If, however, your standard deviation was two, your control limits would broaden to 14 and two. In other words, the higher the standard deviation is, the greater the variability will be in your process's performance.

Relax. You don't need to understand the theoretical concept of standard deviation to use control charts, but, if you're interested, a brief explanation is provided on page 87 (figure 5-9). You should know, however, that the laws of statistical probability enable you to feel very confident about the accuracy of your control limits. For a normal distribution — and most distributions resulting from real processes are normal — 99.7 percent of the data will fall within three standard deviations above or below the center line. You can, therefore, safely assume that points falling outside the control limits indicate the presence of abnormal variation.

Constructing Control Charts

There are still a few things you need to know before constructing your first control chart. Keep in mind that performance data may be categorized as either variable or attribute. *Variable data*, also known as measurement data, consist of observations that can vary along a continuum. Examples of variable data are times of day, temperatures, and weights. *Attribute data* consist of counts and values based on counts. While variable data are a measure of something that's more or less than something else, attribute data are a measure of something that simply is or is not correct, on time, within specifications, etc. Attribute data can represent either individual counts of things — the numbers of defects in a product, for example — or a proportion, such as the percentage of defective items contained in a shipment of goods.

Variable and attribute data each require the use of different kinds of control charts. There are four kinds of control charts you can use:

1. Sample averages ($\overline{X}$) and sample ranges (R) chart

2. Individual values (X) and moving ranges (MR) chart

3. Proportion defective (p) chart

4. Individual or counted defects (c) chart

Both the $\overline{X}$ and R chart and the X and MR chart are used with variable data, and, in each case, two charts are actually computed.

The averages ($\overline{X}$ or X) chart illustrates variation over time, which is referred to as long-term variation. The ranges (R or MR) chart illustrates variation at a fixed point in time, which is referred to as short-term variation.

Both p charts and c charts are used with attribute data. When using either one, you'll need only to construct one chart. As the names suggest, a p chart is used when your data are presented as a proportion or a percentage defective, and a c chart is used when your data are presented as individual or counted defects.

Detailed guidelines for using each kind of control chart are provided on pages 167-190 in the Toolbox. In general, however, the major steps for constructing a control chart, regardless of which kind you use, are:

1. Calculate the basic statistics (for example, range, average, or proportion) that you'll need to establish control limits.

2. Scale and label each axis, as you would when using a run chart. As you can see from the commuting example (figure 5-8 on page 83), the vertical axis is scaled from 14 to 26 and labeled "commuting time" (in minutes). The horizontal axis is scaled to show work days for a four-week period. There's nothing difficult about this step: Simply scale the chart based on the range for your data.

3. Compute your control limits and draw control lines on your chart.

4. Plot your data.

5. Identify any abnormal variation.

6. Eliminate abnormal variation and recompute the control limits.

Figure 5-9
**Standard Deviation –
Quantifying Variation**

The standard deviation is an efficient way of expressing the spread of a group of numbers or data. You'll remember from the last chapter that range is a way of measuring spread. But as a group of numbers gets larger, range becomes less useful because, as shown below, it cannot distinguish between very different data distributions.

These two sets of data have the same number of points, the same average, and the same range, but they look very different. In fact, they are different because the distribution on the right has a greater spread than the one on the left. This is so because more points are located further from the average value in that distribution.

```
              X
          X   X   X
          X   X   X                           X   X   X
      X   X   X   X   X               X   X   X   X   X   X   X   X   X
  X   X   X   X   X   X   X   X   X       X   X   X   X   X   X   X   X   X
 ─────────────────────────────        ──────────────────────────────
 16  17  18  19  20  21  22  23  24    16  17  18  19  20  21  22  23  24
```

While this observation is accurate, however, it is not precise. In order to be precise, we must be able to accurately measure the spread of a distribution. This can be done by computing the standard deviation as follows:

1. Determine the average value for the distribution:

$$\overline{X} = (X_1 + X_2 + X_3 ... + X_n)/n$$

2. Determine the distance between each point in the distribution and the distribution average. Square each result, add the results, and divide by the total (X_n) in order to compute a statistic known as the variance (v). The formula is as follows:

$$v = \frac{[(X_1 - \overline{X})^2 + (X_2 - \overline{X})^2 + (X_3 - \overline{X})^2 ... + (X_n - \overline{X})^2]}{n}$$

3. To compute the standard deviation(s), simply determine the square root of the variance as follows:

$$s = \frac{\sqrt{(X_1 - \overline{X})^2 + (X_2 - \overline{X})^2 + (X_3 - \overline{X})^2 ... + (X_n - \overline{X})^2}}{n}$$

In the example above, the standard deviation for the distribution on the left is 1.88; for the distribution on the right, it is 2.41. The standard deviation is an accurate and, therefore, more useful method for measuring the spread of a distribution.

Figure 5-10
Decision Tree for Control Chart Selection

Selecting the Right Control Chart

The flowchart shown on this page (figure 5-10) will help you select the control chart you need, based on your data. To clarify this further, here's an example of the circumstances under which each kind of control chart might be used.

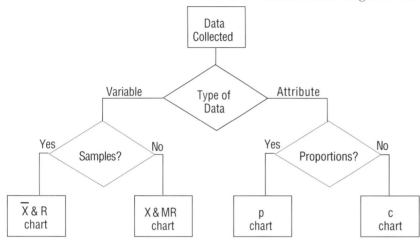

Let's assume that, within the financial management division of an organization, a team is working to improve the invoice payment process. The team collected data for the following four measures:

- time it takes to pay an invoice (in days)

- over- and underpayments (in dollars)

- missing or misfiled receiving reports (as a proportion of the total invoices processed)

- amount of downtime in the financial management computer system (computed as hours down each month)

Note that the first two measurements (number of days and dollars) contain variable data, while the last two (misplaced reports and defective computer time) contain attribute data.

Luckily, the team learned that information on the dollar value of mispayments and computer downtime that occurred each week was readily available in the organization's data files. As a result, the team was able to quantify those two measurements on a weekly basis for as far back as they wished.

However, information on the time needed to pay individual invoices and the number of times receiving reports were missing had not been previously recorded. So, the team developed a measurement plan that directed them to collect the data they needed over a 20-working-day period.

Each of the four measurements the team decided to collect data on required use of a different type of control chart. Refer back to the flowchart (figure 5-10) on page 88. As you do so, notice that:

- Time to pay invoices is variable data and can be sampled. Therefore, the control chart for sample averages ($\overline{X}$ and R chart) is the right one to use in this case.

- Dollar value of over- and underpayments is variable data. Since the team wished to capture the total dollar value, not a sample of it, they did not use samples. Instead, they used a control chart for individual data (X and MR chart).

- Data that categorize receiving reports as "missing" or "not missing" are attribute data. In this case, the team thought it best to express the attribute as a proportion of the total number of invoices processed, all of which required receiving reports. Therefore, it used a p chart.

- Data pertaining to computer downtime are also attribute data. The team wanted a chart that showed the number, not proportion, of hours of downtime, so they used a c chart.

In Control vs. Out of Control

To use a control chart to identify and understand variation in your process, you must be able to determine if the process is or is not in control. How do you do that? By understanding that a process is said to be in control when it exhibits only normal variation. In contrast, a process is said to be out of control when abnormal variation is also present. Notice also that how much variation there is in a process has nothing to do with whether it's in control or not.

In the control chart shown on page 90 (figure 5-11), no unusual cycles or trends are apparent. The data appear to fluctuate randomly within the upper and lower control limits. Since it exhibits only normal variation, this process is in control.

Figure 5-11

Control Chart of "In-Control" Process

The control chart on page 91(figure 5-12) tells a different story. It exhibits five distinct characteristics, each of which indicates the presence of abnormal variation. Each shaded area is numbered to correspond to the following observations:

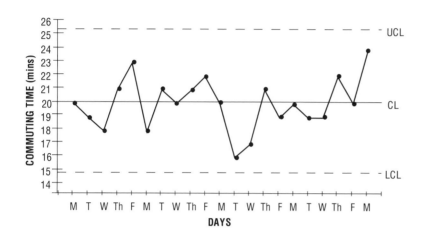

1. These two points are outside the control limits — one above, the other below. This, as has been already discussed, is an obvious indication of abnormal variation.

2. This grouping represents a trend, as indicated by the fact that seven points in a row move in one direction. In this example, as you can see, the trend is upward.

3. These groupings indicate a process average shift, which describes a situation where seven points in a row appear either above or below the center line. This pattern indicates that fundamental change has occurred in this process. At this point, the team would have to recalculate the chart's control lines.

4. This grouping displays what is known as "hugging the center line." Groupings are said to hug the center line when seven consecutive points appear in the middle third of the area between your control limits.

5. This last grouping displays what is known as "hugging the control limits." That occurs when either two out of three, three out of seven, or four out of 10 points appear in the outer one third of the area between your control limits. In this example, two out of three consecutive points display this characteristic.

Control Abnormal Variation

If, after charting the performance of your process, you find that there's evidence of abnormal variation, what should you do about it? Two things — investigate it and remove it.

Investigate the reasons for abnormal variation by looking for special causes in the records that are associated with the data, time, shift, or lot number indicated on your run or control chart. When trends and process shifts are involved, focus your investigation on what was going on when the pattern began.

Once you have discovered the special causes for your abnormal variation, you must decide what action, if any, to take. For example, if you were an hour late for work because of an accident, you might acknowledge this special cause and conclude that it's a rare occurrence that must be tolerated. If, on the other hand, ongoing road construction caused your delay, you may decide to choose a new route until the construction is completed.

After addressing the causes for abnormal variation, you'll need to recalculate your control limits. Keep in mind that the presence of abnormal variation masks the true performance of your process. You must, therefore, eliminate the influence of abnormal variation by establishing new control limits. The new limits, which will be based on only normal variation, will finally provide an accurate picture of what your process is currently capable of achieving.

Key Action 2: Evaluate Current Performance

This simple but important step will enable you to further focus your improvement effort. To evaluate current performance, you must

Figure 5-12
Control Chart of "Out-of-Control" Process

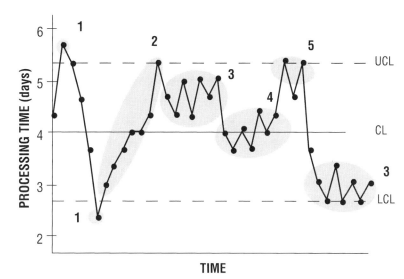

know two things: how the process is currently performing and how it needs to perform. When you identify gaps between actual performance and the performance customers expect, you can then look for causes to explain those gaps. This is, in essence, the beginning of problem-solving.

After charting and analyzing your performance data, you should have a good understanding of how your process is currently performing. To determine how it needs to perform to meet customer expectations, however, you may need to consider the following issues:

- Do you have a contract that establishes performance requirements?

- Does your organization have a policy that establishes performance expectations?

- Do specifications exist?

- Is there a precedent that has created customer expectations? Let's say, for example, that you've been delivering a level of service that customers have come to expect. That level of service, in your customers' minds, has established a precedent against which all future performance will be measured.

- Have competitors created a new performance baseline? When Federal Express introduced overnight delivery service, for example, the company essentially created new customer expectations for mail service that affected all mail carriers.

Once you've established your process's expected or desired performance, using whatever criteria are appropriate, you can evaluate current performance by comparing the "as is" with the "should be" performance levels. The invoice payment team, for example, would compare an average time to pay invoices of 45 days, plus or minus eight, with a policy that requires invoices to be paid within 30 days.

The comparisons you make during this step will enable you to identify significant performance gaps, not just at the customer expectation level, but at the output characteristic level as well. It's one thing, for example, to know that too many cups are leaking. It's another thing, however, to know that cups are leaking because of problems related to gluing the seams.

Once you've identified significant performance gaps, the next step is to list and prioritize potential causes for these gaps that, from the team's perspective, are problem areas they can investigate and improve.

Evaluating Process Performance

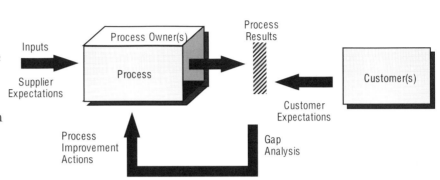

Key Action 3: Prioritize Problem Areas

This action consists primarily of listing causes for specific performance problems, discussing them as a team, and isolating the causes your team believes are most significant. Review the results of the efforts you've already made to chart and evaluate current performance. You may also find useful insights in the notes you've taken during customer interviews. If you're not sure, talk to a few more process managers and/or employees to develop as complete a picture as you can. You can also use process flowcharts to help you identify causes and Pareto diagrams to help you prioritize them.

Process Flow Analysis

When you were defining your process, your team answered some basic questions about your process such as: What steps occur? Who does what? In what order do things happen? Why do you perform each step? Where do you perform each step?

By answering such questions, you gathered important information and insights that helped you describe the process. Now you can begin to build on the information you included in earlier flowcharts and answer more probing questions that will help you identify causes for poor performance. Once you have a list of potential causes you can then prioritize them, determine their root causes, and develop solutions.

Helpful Hint

Before you develop a flowchart from scratch, check to see if one already exists. It's easier to update an existing flowchart than to construct a new one.

A detailed flowchart is an excellent tool for analyzing process flow. In fact, it will also be useful later on, when you're studying problems in even greater detail. Remember not to create any unnecessary work for yourselves, however. Before you develop a flowchart from scratch, check to see if one already exists. It's easier to update and confirm an existing flowchart than it is to construct a new one. Refer to pages 193-194 of the Toolbox for more information on how to develop and use detailed flowcharts.

Remember to analyze the process flow in light of your process's existing performance problems. If a significant performance gap involves cycle time, for example, look for problems that contribute to delays or bottlenecks. If quality is an area of concern, identify problems that come from errors, omissions, or substandard performance.

Pareto Diagrams

Pareto diagrams are a great help when you're attempting to prioritize the causes you've identified. A Pareto diagram is simply a bar graph. Each bar generally represents a problem or cause of a problem. The height of each bar indicates the frequency or significance of the problem or cause under scrutiny. The bars are arranged from left to right in descending order of importance.

A Pareto diagram graphically illustrates the "vital few" issues that frequently account for most of the trouble occurring in a process. It visually depicts what's commonly known as the 80-20 rule, which states that the source of a given problem can often be traced to 20 percent of its potential causes. By isolating these "vital few" causes, a Pareto diagram can direct your efforts to the real areas of opportunity for improvement that exist in your process.

To use a Pareto diagram, you must have data. As a team, discuss and agree on what information you need and where to find it. Then, if necessary, design a checksheet and collect your data. Refer to pages 213-215 of the Toolbox for guidelines on how to develop Pareto diagrams.

Once you've completed the activities described in this chapter, you'll embark on what may be the most rewarding phase of your improvement effort: developing solutions. The next chapter will facilitate that journey.

Chapter 6

DEVELOP SOLUTIONS

Getting Ready to Solve Problems

Finally, it's time to start fixing things! This chapter is all about solving problems — a challenge you confront every day.

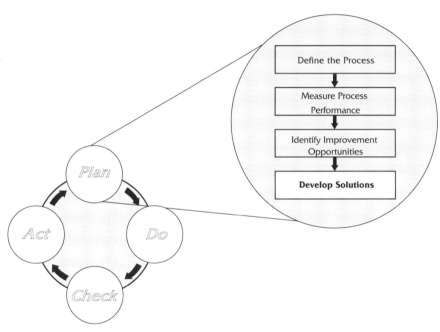

But problem-solving in a quality environment may be very different from what you're used to. The guidelines provided in this chapter are designed to help your team really solve problems instead of just fighting fires.

Effective problem-solving employs the right people and a systematic approach to uncover the root causes of problems. Uncovering those root causes will enable you to solve the right problems — the ones that cause unsatisfactory performance in areas important to your customers. And where will that lead? You've guessed it: to improved customer satisfaction.

Keep in mind, however, that meaningful improvement may require more than solving the problems that directly affect your process. Your team must also look for opportunities to make satisfactory process performance even better — provided, of course, that such improvements will enhance customer satisfaction.

Figure 6-1

Keys to Success

It takes more than a systematic method to identify meaningful process improvements. Your team's success will also depend on effective teamwork (see Chapter II) and a lion's share of creative thinking efforts.

To come up with new, innovative ideas for solving problems and improving processes, you must work at it. There are tools available to promote creative thinking, but your attitude is crucial.

You must be willing, for example, to challenge accepted ways of doing things — the boundaries that define the limits of what's permissible — even your own assumptions about what is and isn't possible. Turn problems upside down. Look at them from varying points of view. This challenging (and childlike) attitude takes practice at first, but as it becomes a habit, you'll find opportunities where you once saw only obstacles.

Look at the figure on this page (figure 6-1). What do you see? If you find the figures strange and meaningless, perhaps you have conditioned yourself to look for meaning only in the black shapes and figures and ignore the white shapes in between. However, if you focus on the white shapes for a moment, you'll soon spot the word "QUALITY."

Now that you've seen the word, look away for a second or two, then look back at the page and try *not* to see it. You cannot. It seems so obvious now that you're probably wondering how you ever missed it.

In a similar manner, you and others around you may harbor well-defined opinions and assumptions about your work problems. Unless your team can focus on those white spaces between the black shapes — on the unconventional as well as the conventional view — you may miss opportunities that are right in front of you.

The rest of this chapter describes a systematic, five-part problem-solving method that instructs you to:

- define the problem

- analyze the problem and determine root causes

- generate improvement ideas

- develop solutions

- present recommendations

These key actions point the way toward meaningful improvements. Some teams will complete all of the actions and use the tools as described. Others will need to tailor the guidelines presented here to reflect their particular situation. To help your team stay on the right track, keep the following guidelines in mind:

Top-Down Flowchart: Process Improvement Method

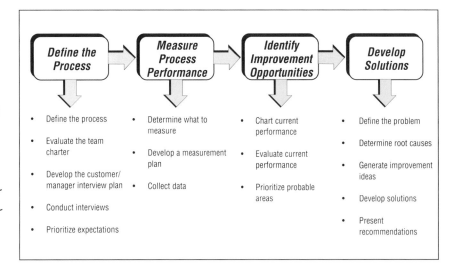

- Your goal is to improve process performance and customer service.

- For each action you take, strive to do only as much as is really necessary.

- Before taking any action, always ask yourselves if it makes sense. If the answer is no, you probably shouldn't do it.

Key Action 1: Define the Problem

In the hope of finding quick solutions, teams are often tempted to rush through the process of defining problems. This well-intentioned haste can lead to frustration and failure. Why? Because teams that hurry through this process often discover that they've found the right solution to the wrong problem or solutions that can't be maintained.

Don't put yourselves in that position! Make the effort required to adequately define your problem — it's time well spent. How much time you'll need will depend on such factors as: whether you already know which problem to focus on, how complex the problem is, how much information you already have, and how available and accessible the data is.

Develop a Problem Statement

Once you're ready to define your problem, it's a good idea to start out by developing a problem statement. There are several reasons for taking this approach. First, in the process of developing a problem statement, you may find out that, at first, your problem appeared more obvious than it turned out to be. Second, team members and stakeholders may view your problem from many different perspectives. You need to develop a problem statement that can help you take advantage of their collective wisdom.

A problem statement can also help you organize what you already know about a problem and identify what you still need to learn. By taking time to *understand* the problem before analyzing it in detail, you can avoid the common pitfalls of traditional problem-solving, such as solving the wrong problem or developing solutions that make sense at your level but don't fit into the bigger picture, and so allow innovative solutions to emerge, instead.

The first step you need to take is to understand the purpose solving your problem will serve. Again, you may think this is obvious, but keep in mind that your initial viewpoint is not the only possible one. It's merely the most apparent one. With a little effort and creative thinking, you can probably identify many reasons for solving your problem.

Brainstorm a "purpose" list. Try to expand the list beyond the obvious. Arrange your list so that the most broadly focused purposes appear first and the most narrowly focused ones appear last, then decide which purpose provides the right focus for your team.

By finding progressively larger purposes for solving your problem, you're forced to challenge the assumptions and self-imposed constraints that people usually bring to looking at a problem. By expanding your focus, you can open the door to many more possible solutions.

Assume, for example, that the coffee-cup team discovered that uneven glue application contributed to leaks at the seam. The obvious purpose for solving this problem is to further secure the seam in order to eliminate such leaks. However, the team might identify other purposes as well, such as reducing the unit cost of paper coffee cups or simply eliminating leaks generally. While the initial purpose may be the right one for this team, a focus on the broader purpose of eliminating leaks might cause them to look at alternatives to paper cups — for instance, styrofoam cups, which have no seams.

Once your team has settled on the right purpose for solving the problem, develop a problem statement. Here's how:

- Write an initial problem definition, but don't over-analyze. Just write down your first impressions. They can be described in a paragraph, a sentence, or even a phrase such as "uneven glue application contributes to leaks."

- List the key players involved. These could include the owners of the problem — that is, those most affected by it or the people who must be involved in decisions to solve the problem.

- Identify controllable variables, the aspects of the problem that decision-makers — such as your team, the process manager, and higher management — can control. The coffee-cup team might identify glue-mixing procedures and machine maintenance schedules as controlling variables.

- Identify uncontrollable variables: the qualitative or quantitative aspects of the problem, such as old mixing or application equipment, that will influence the outcome but that probably can't be controlled by key players.

- Identify constraints. These are the limitations, such as the

Figure 6-2

Problem Definition Checklist

Why is it necessary to solve this problem?

What benefits can we hope to realize by solving this problem?

What do we know about the problem?

What is it that we don't yet understand?

What information do we already have that is related to this problem?

What additional information must we acquire before proceeding further?

What additional information would be nice to have?

Can the problem be divided into parts?

How long has the problem existed?

Is it persistent? Chronic?

Can we solve the whole problem? Part of the problem?

---

availability of data, that will affect your analysis of the problem or any solutions you may devise. The coffee-cup team, for example, may be constrained by a strategic decision to stick with paper coffee cups. Constraints can exist at your level (local), at the organizational level, or even externally (global). Look to your charter for guidance. Get clarification from management if you're unclear about what your constraints are.

• List possible outcomes, then review your list of purposes. Brainstorm some possible solutions. Think of the future implications of your solutions. Look beyond your immediate situation to the next solution. Consider the potential outcome of the solutions you identify, such as the good things that may be achieved or the bad things that may be avoided.

Why look for future solutions to current problems? The answer is simple: You'll save yourself the headaches that short-term fixes inevitably cause. Looking for the ideal solution, even if it exists in the future, opens up your thinking to new possibilities. It enables you to head toward the future instead of backing away from the past.

The Problem Checklist

As you define, analyze, and ultimately solve your problem, you will constantly ask and answer questions. Years ago, the CIA developed a technique for doing this that's known as Phoenix. The Problem Definition Checklist on page 102 (figure 6-2) is an adaptation of the Phoenix checklist, which was originally designed to help agents look at a problem from many different perspectives. Add questions to the list as you go along.

Focusing on the facts instills a sense of team discipline that will help you understand what causes problems before you repair them. That way, the right things get fixed!

Key Action 2: Analyze the Problem

By thoroughly defining your problem, you have successfully avoided the pitfalls of "analysis first" problem-solving. If detailed analysis is necessary (and it often is), now is the time to begin this work.

You'll probably need to collect some data and use a few basic TQM tools to help you really understand your problem. Remember the guidance provided at the beginning of this chapter: Do only as much as necessary. The amount of work you absolutely need to do will depend on the problem you analyze, but generally you should complete the following steps:

- locate the problem

- describe the problem

- determine the root causes of the problem

Tips on Collecting Cause Data

Asking you to collect more data may seem like too much work — especially since you already know a lot about the process, and you're understandably anxious to fix certain problems. Remember, though, that getting the added information you need is just as important as collecting the initial information. Focusing on the facts instills a sense of team discipline that will help you develop a clear understanding of what causes problems before you repair them. That way, the right things get fixed!

Remember that collecting data should always be seen as a step toward some future action, not as just an exercise. Don't let it overwhelm you. When deciding what data to collect, always consider carefully what the data will reveal and how difficult they will be to collect. You may wish to refer back to Chapter IV for such helpful data collection techniques as sampling, using checksheets, and developing a measurement plan.

Process Flow Analysis

One of the ways you can begin to uncover the root causes of your problem is by viewing it in the context of the process flow. A detailed flowchart can help you do this because it shows your process as it "really is" instead of as it "should be." If you developed a detailed flowchart earlier to help you identify problems, use it now to focus your team's attention on the problem you want to solve.

If you haven't already developed a detailed flowchart, consider doing so now. It will help the team think through what really happens in your process. You'll know the tool is working once the team begins to ask (and eventually answer) many questions.

Remember that you often need data to answer some of these questions. Resist the temptation to assume you know the answer and move on, if what the team really needs is new information. To quote Sherlock Holmes, "There's nothing so dangerous as an obvious fact."

As you examine the process flow, try to determine where the problem begins and which parts of your process (and perhaps other processes as well) it affects the most. Does the problem begin in your process? Does it enter your process from an upstream process? This often happens because the internal customer-supplier relationship is not clearly understood; problems often get moved from one place to another instead of solved. Try not to make the same mistake.

Next, determine how the problem exhibits itself. What are the results you can see and measure? Your flowchart should reveal delays, sources of errors, bottlenecks, rework, etc. Discussing the chart may even lead you to discover that extra inspections, process steps, or even entire jobs have been created just to clean up the mess that existing problems create.

Be sure to ask probing questions to help your team accurately describe the problem and uncover its potential causes. Here are some questions to get you started:

- How many errors are there?

- How often does the problem occur?

- When does the problem occur? At all hours? Only during peak hours or seasons?

- How long are the delays that are involved?

- What does the problem cost?

- Why does this happen?

- Who is affected? How?

Streamlining a Process

Streamlining the Process

The process flow is difficult to analyze without beginning to identify potential solutions. It's O.K. to discuss streamlining related ideas at this point, but be careful not to settle on improvements prematurely. Streamlining and automating a process frequently can improve process performance in terms of throughput

Before Streamlining

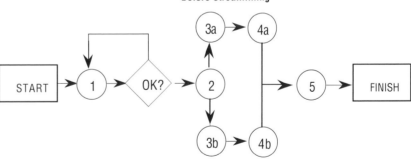

After Streamlining

Finding root causes is worth the effort. Fixing symptoms instead of problems usually provides temporary – not permanent – improvement.

time, cost, accuracy, etc. However, the problem often must be solved *before* it can be effectively streamlined.

For example, let's suppose that the supervisor of a process spends most of her time inspecting the work of her staff. She does this because, when mistakes go out the door, the boss gets furious. That inspection process can be streamlined or eliminated only when the problems that cause mistakes are solved.

As your team generates ideas to improve the process flow, write them on 3" x 5" index cards and place them in an "idea box." You can revisit them later. That way, you don't lose track of good ideas — and you also don't compromise your systematic problem-solving approach.

Why do this? Well, in response to a crisis, people often succeed only in making a process more complex. As a result, an immediate solution that may complicate the process, such as an added inspection or approval requirement, often outlives the problem that brought it about. Over time, people close to the process wind up getting used to the additional steps and may not see them as obstacles. Keep this in mind as you analyze the problem, but don't take action yet.

As you look for ways to improve the process flow, however, continue to ask questions like the ones below:

- Do we actually use all the information on that form?

- Why do we require three approval signatures?

- Why do we send a copy of the results to every department?

- Why is the process laid out this way?

- What would it take to eliminate this step?

Root Cause Analysis

Your team must discover the root causes of problems in order to identify lasting improvements. Sometimes that sounds easier than it is. That's because root causes can get lost in a maze of overlapping problems, secondary causes, and symptoms. Untangling the mess often requires time, energy, and special tools.

But finding root causes is worth the effort. Fixing symptoms instead of problems usually provides only temporary improvement. If you take pain killers for a toothache, for example, are you attacking the root cause of the pain? It's not likely. You may find some temporary relief, but a permanent solution requires a visit to the dentist.

To identify root causes, you must untangle the maze of symptoms and intermediate causes by systematic probing. You must learn to ask "why" repeatedly. This comes naturally to children, but adults sometimes tend to give up too soon.

There's a rule of thumb common to many problem-solving methods that says you must ask (and answer) the "why" question up to five times before you reach the root cause of a problem. Here's an excerpt from Yuzo Yasuda's recent book on the Toyota production system, *40 Years, 20 Million Ideas: The Toyota Suggestion System*, that introduces a way to do this:

Question	Answer
1. Why did the machine break?	It became overloaded and blew a fuse.
2. Why did it overload?	The lubrication failed.
3. Why did the lubrication fail?	The pump malfunctioned.
4. Why did it malfunction?	The pump axle wore out prematurely.
5. Why did it wear out?	Dirt got inside the pump.

Figure 6-3
Linked Pareto Diagrams

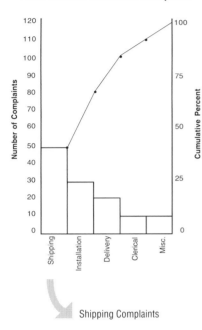

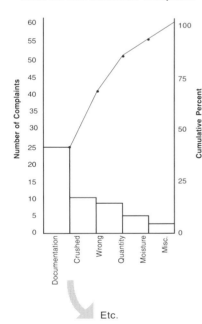

If the team studying this machine failure had stopped asking "why" after they had answered the first question, it would have merely replaced the fuse — a temporary solution at best. By asking "why" repeatedly, it eventually discovered that the real solution to the problem was to attach a filter to the lubricating pump to keep the dust and dirt out.

Three quality tools are especially helpful in identifying the root causes of your problem: Pareto diagrams, cause-and-effect diagrams, and scatter diagrams.

Using Pareto Diagrams to Isolate Root Causes

You've already discovered that Pareto diagrams are a useful tool for identifying key problems. By linking a series of increasingly detailed Pareto diagrams together, however, you can also uncover the root cause of your problem. The example shown on this page (figure 6-3) shows how linked Pareto diagrams can be used to uncover the root causes of customer complaints.

The advantage of this technique lies in its objectivity. Since Pareto diagrams rely on data, the causal relationships you establish through the use of them should be solid. The disadvantage of the Pareto diagram is its lack of flexibility. While a team can decide spontaneously during a meeting to use a cause-and-effect diagram to explore a problem's root causes, this is not practical using linked Pareto diagrams. Data collection that's required to create Pareto diagrams takes time and is, therefore, best done between meetings.

Your team can use linked Pareto diagrams to confirm initial assumptions developed using a cause-and-effect diagram. Discuss potential causes, determine performance issues, and design checksheets during a team meeting. Then collect data prior to the next meeting, when the team can develop linked Pareto diagrams together.

Using Cause-and-Effect Diagrams

Perhaps the most useful tool for identifying root causes is the *cause-and-effect diagram*, shown on this page (figure 6-4). It goes by several names and there are a variety of ways to use it, but the cause-and-effect diagram is primarily a tool for organizing information to establish and clarify the relationships between an effect and its main causes, between a main cause and its secondary causes, and so on.

The cause-and-effect diagram is an extremely flexible tool and can be adapted to almost any situation. While this tool is easy to understand conceptually, our experience has been that teams sometimes find it difficult to use at first. Don't lose patience. Many teams discover that, with a little practice, the cause and effect diagram quickly becomes the most versatile and useful TQM tool.

As you can see from the example shown below on this page (figure 6-5), the invoice payment team has collected and organized a lot of information, using a cause-and-effect diagram, to help them understand why invoices are paid late. The reasons are more complex than the team members originally thought. For example, internal mail problems appear to stem from inexperienced staff, old equipment, and

Figure 6-4

Cause-and-Effect Diagram

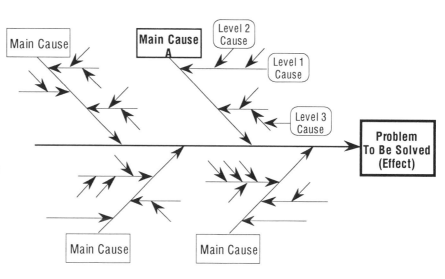

Figure 6-5

Cause-and-Effect Diagram (Invoice Payment Process)

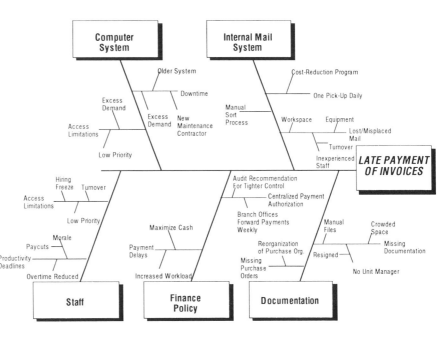

manual sorting processes that are appropriate only for much lower volume levels.

The following cause-and-effect diagram guidelines will give you a sense of what's involved in creating one. For a more detailed discussion of this tool, however, see pages 160-162 of the Toolbox.

- Get ideas from as many people as possible. Continuously ask yourselves and others, "What causes this?"

- Use a cause-and-effect diagram to keep a discussion focused on a specific topic and to avoid repetition of complaints and grievances.

- The relationship between any cause and its effects usually consists of many complex elements that are interrelated on a variety of levels. If your diagram looks like the one shown on this page (figure 6-6), you're not there yet. Do you know enough about the problem? If not, find people who *do* know enough and get them to help you. Ask questions, interview key people, use available networks, and collect data.

Figure 6-6
**Incomplete Cause-
and-Effect Diagram**

Using Scatter Diagrams

Complex problems often require that you verify a relationship between a cause and its effect or a relationship between two causes. A *scatter diagram* can tell you if a relationship exists and, if so, how strong it is. This can help you avoid recommending the wrong solution. It may also provide management with the proof it needs to implement a controversial or costly solution. For more information about scatter diagrams, turn to pages 223-225 of the Toolbox.

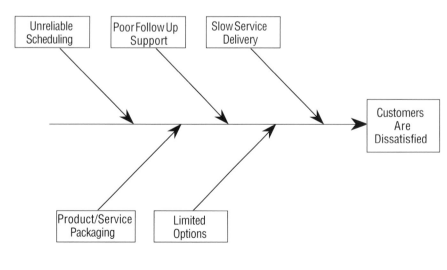

Let's return to the coffee-cup team to illustrate how a scatter diagram might work. Let's assume that the team has focused on the wax coating, which is not uniformly applied, as a cause for leaks. Through additional analysis, the team isolated variation in the conveyor belt speed as the potential root cause of uneven wax coating application.

Figure 6-7
Scatter Diagram

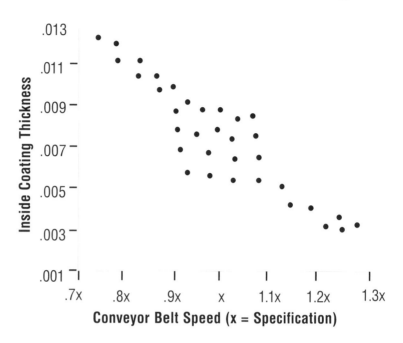

But they weren't sure. To test this hypothesis, the team collected a sample of cups at random from the line every 30 minutes for an entire week. During that time, they measured the conveyor belt speed and the wax coating thickness of each sample they selected. At the end of the week, they plotted the results on a scatter diagram, as shown on this page (figure 6-7).

Teams frequently avoid scatter diagrams because they're thought to be complicated or unnecessary. In fact, they serve as an excellent complement to cause-and-effect diagrams. What's more, the median method recommended here is a simple (and non-statistical) alternative method for determining the relationship between two variables.

Think of a cause-and-effect diagram as a tool that helps your team develop a hypothesis about a problem's causes and effects. A scatter diagram enables you to test your hypothesis and either confirm or disprove it. Effective use of scatter diagrams can lead to conclusions based on facts, not guesswork.

Obstacles	Guidelines for Surmounting Them
1. Root causes aren't easy to find	• challenge initial assumptions • be persistent • follow the improvement process • seek input from as many sources as possible
2. Pressure for quick solutions	• be patient — don't jump to conclusions • manage management's expectations • don't overlook easy opportunities • communicate interim results to outsiders (managers, customers, stakeholders, etc.)
3. Preconceived notions about problems and causes	• let data reveal the true picture • bring out and explore dissenting views • challenge assumptions — treat your problem as unique • use analytical tools
4. Resistance to collecting more data	• look for data that is already available • collect data intelligently — look for opportunities to collect cause data during initial data collection efforts • distribute the workload evenly among all team members • plan data collection — use good check-sheets and collect the right data the first time

Up until now, you've learned about methods for handling just one kind of data at a time. Scatter diagrams show the relationship between what's known as paired data. For example, figure 6-7, shown on page 111, seeks to determine if there's a relationship between the inside coating thickness of the cups and the speed at which the conveyor belt operates. The diagram shows that there is no relationship between the thickness of the cups' inside coating and conveyor belt speed when the conveyor is operating at normal (specification) speed.

A relationship between coating thickness and conveyor belt speed does exist, however, when the conveyor belt travels at less than 90 percent or more than 110 percent of its normal speed.

To use a scatter diagram effectively, you must first identify the variables to be studied. You then collect data, plot the data on a graph, test for a relationship, and build results into your conclusions and recommendations. When testing for a relationship, there are five basic possibilities, as shown on page 113 (figure 6-8).

Tips for Successful Root Cause Analysis

So far, this chapter has explained why it's important to uncover root causes and has demonstrated how Pareto charts, cause-and-effect diagrams, and scatter diagrams can help. As useful as these tools

Figure 6-8
Five Different Scatter Diagram Results

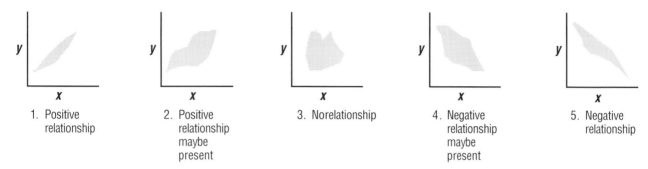

1. Positive relationship
2. Positive relationship maybe present
3. Norelationship
4. Negative relationship maybe present
5. Negative relationship

are, they cannot work if your team starts to cut corners. The pressures to do so can originate from inside or outside the team. You can take steps to avoid giving into this pressure by examining the potential obstacles to successful root cause analysis and guidelines for surmounting them outlined on page 112.

Confirming Your Assumptions

Now that you've determined the root causes of your problem, your team is ready to develop solutions. If you are at all uncertain about the cause-and-effect relationship you've established, it's a good idea to verify that relationship before proceeding.

Figure 6-9
Tree Diagram

One way to do this is to develop a *tree diagram*. Also known as a systematic diagram, the tree diagram was developed to search for the most effective means of accomplishing a given objective. It's called a tree diagram because it represents information in a way that resembles the branches of a tree. This representation helps clarify the relationship between either an objective and the means for achieving it or between a cause and its effects.

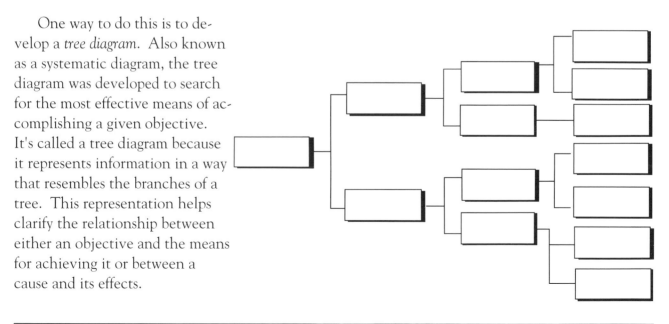

Figure 6-10
**Tree Diagram –
Coffee Cup Team**

Figure 6-9 on page 113 shows a generic example of the shape a tree diagram can take. The illustration on page 114 (figure 6-10) is a partially completed example of the tree diagram that the coffee-cup team might develop. It identifies one of the root causes of leaky cups as inadequate machine maintenance schedules.

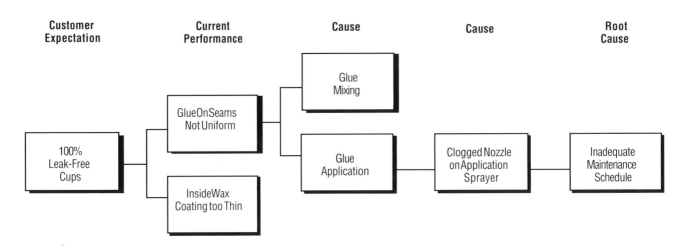

Refer to pages 230-231 of the Toolbox to help you develop and use a tree diagram to test your assumptions. It doesn't take much time, and it can sometimes help you avoid developing the right solution to the wrong problem.

Key Action 3: Generate Improvement Ideas

In TQM literature, a lot of emphasis is placed on the value of taking a systematic approach to problem-solving, making data-driven decisions, establishing a customer focus, and developing process thinking. These are routinely listed as critical to team success.

Still, the importance of ideas is too often understated. Ultimately, your team's success will depend on your ability to recommend innovative solutions — an ability that requires a combination of analytical thinking and creative thinking.

Analytical thinking may come naturally to most of us, while creative thinking may not. The good news is that creative thinking can be learned. Practice the techniques described throughout this book. Use the tools. With hard work and a little patience, your team will create lots of ideas that will result in real solutions.

Tips for Successful Idea Generation

There are literally hundreds of easy-to-use techniques and tools that can help your team create lots of good ideas. Make up your own. Experiment with different approaches. Some useful tips to get you started are listed below.

Write Your Ideas Down

You never know when a good idea will come to you. Often, they first emerge as vague beginnings of a new idea and are easily forgotten. Capture ideas on paper (or in a computer) and you won't lose them.

Distribute idea notes to all team members. Keep an "idea box." You can use this technique to keep the team on track when a good idea comes up at the wrong time. Your idea box can serve as a source of energy when ideas are slow to come to you.

Avoid Idea Assassins

Creativity flourishes in a positive, open environment. Many good ideas are thrown away before they have time to develop because of negative thinking. "Idea assassins" are the familiar phrases that many people use to express hostility to ideas and resist change.

Here are some examples of common idea assassins. It's a good idea to ban phrases like these from team discussions during idea generation sessions:

- "Yes, but..."

- "We've tried that before."

- "That may work somewhere else but not here."

- "It'll never fly."

- "The boss won't buy it."

- "We've always done it this way."

- "It sounds O.K. in theory but..."

Osborn's Brain-storming Rules

- No criticism. Don't evaluate ideas during idea generation.

- No constraints. Take a freewheeling approach. It's welcome, even preferred — the wilder the idea, the better. It's easier to tame ideas than to make them more and more outrageous.

- Go for quantity. Generate as many ideas as possible. More ideas increase the odds of good ideas emerging.

- Build on existing ideas. Don't leave an idea alone because someone else came up with it. Use one idea to create others. Combine and improve them.

- "The regulations won't let us do that."

- "It's against procedures."

Adhere to Osborn's Brainstorming Rules

Brainstorming is also a great and popular technique for generating ideas. Many ways to conduct brainstorming sessions have been developed over the years. Unfortunately, however, this technique is often misused in ways that greatly reduce its effectiveness.

Nominal group technique is used to generate ideas. It's generally recommended for groups of people who have just met, because while it doesn't require a lot of personal interaction, it gets the group involved in the idea generating and prioritization process. For more information on how to conduct a session using nominal group technique, see pages 207-208 of the Toolbox.

Whether you're brainstorming or using some other idea-generation technique, it's best to follow the simple brainstorming rules contained in Alex Osborn's *Applied Imagination, Principles and Procedures of Creative Thinking*, and let the ideas flow. A sample of these rules is included on this page, but more specific brainstorming guidelines appear on pages 157-159 of the Toolbox.

Challenge Assumptions

Everyone brings assumptions to the problem-solving table. Such assumptions can reflect what we know or, as is often the case, what we think we know. Challenging conventional assumptions about your problem can help you turn obstacles into opportunities. For more information on a specific technique you can use to challenge assumptions, see pages 163-164 of the Toolbox.

Vary Your Perspective

There's an old adage that says, "What you see depends on where you stand." To avoid the dangers of tunnel vision, look at your

Figure 6-11
Solution Map

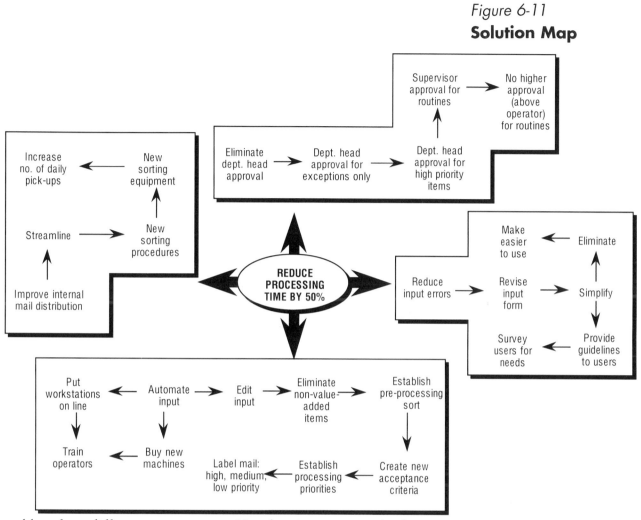

problem from different perspectives: Your boss's, a customer's, the president of your company's.

Put yourselves in their shoes. Imagine what the problem would look like to them. Describe the problem from their perspective. Jot down new ideas that emerge from looking at things this way.

Build Solution Maps

This technique combines traditional systematic, focused analytical thinking with spontaneous, unconstrained thinking. The objective is to create more and better ideas. Building a *solution map* involves a type of structured brainstorming that encourages what author, consultant, and creativity expert Charles "Chic" Thompson calls the "Ready, Fire, Aim" approach to idea generation.

Solution maps involve all team members and are fun to use. Start with a core premise that can be stated as either an objective or a challenge. In the example shown on page 117(figure 6-11), the map started with a goal of reducing processing time by 50 percent.

Using the principles of brainstorming, one person offers an idea and other team members try to expand it, give it a new twist, or turn it into another idea. As the session progresses, clusters of related ideas form around the core premise.

You literally build a solution map as you go so the team can see its ideas begin to take shape. It's important, therefore, that everyone is able to see the solution map as it is being developed. Use a dry-erase board or tape flipchart paper on a wall and use "sticky notes" to record individual ideas. See pages 226-227 of the Toolbox for more about this technique.

Visualize an Ideal Solution

Don't underestimate the value of intuitive techniques that tap into your subconscious and find ideas you didn't know you had. There are many intuitive idea-generating techniques such as relaxation, mental imagery, and visualization.

These techniques facilitate the creative process. They help you to visualize connections between previously unrelated concepts, to move information from one context to another, and to gain insights that lead to new ideas. The inspiration for the hypodermic needle, for example, came from observing rattlesnakes; they inject their victims with venom through a hole running down the center of a tooth — just like hypodermics do. Albert Einstein, to cite another example, wrote that he didn't discover the theory of relativity using math or language; the principles of relativity came to him in a visual image.

Idealized redesign is a creative visualization technique that can be used to broaden the team's perspective on a problem. Instead of seeking solutions to escape an undesirable present, idealized redesign describes an ideal solution that exists in the future.

You've heard the old expression "what you don't know can't hurt you." Well, in traditional problem-solving, what you do know can hurt you by limiting what you see, feel, and think. Idealized redesign allows your team to focus only on the ideal characteristics of your solution and escape constraints that exist in the present. By temporarily putting aside all concerns about existing procedures, assumptions, and limitations, your team can often visualize solutions that would never have surfaced if you had only tried to fix the current situation. For more details on idealized redesign, see pages 203-205 of the Toolbox.

Key Action 4: Develop Solutions

It's nice to think of ideas free from the constraints of the real world. But before you can translate ideas into solutions, you must first subject them to intense scrutiny. Now is the time to put your analytical hat back on and evaluate the ideas you've generated so far.

As you begin this process, keep in mind that your objective is to present recommendations to management that represent the very best ideas your team has to offer. To achieve this objective, complete the following steps:

- Determine the criteria you'll use to evaluate your ideas.

- Evaluate your ideas.

- Rank your ideas.

- Decide which of your ideas you'll present as recommendations.

- Suggest ongoing process-monitoring measures.

During the process of completing these steps, ask yourselves the following questions:

- What will the best solutions look like?

Use all the sources of information you can find to determine what your evaluation criteria should be:

- Take another look at your customer interview notes

- Review your charter

- Talk to customers, managers, or other interested stakeholders

Figure 6-12
Force Field Analysis

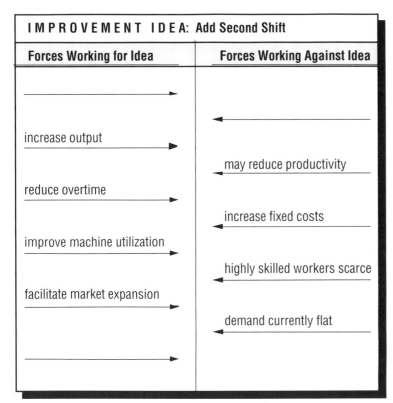

- Which of the best solutions will be the cheapest to implement?

- Which solutions will be the most dramatic? The most visible?

- Which will show the fastest results — deliver the most "bang for the buck"?

- Which will meet the least resistance and be the easiest to put in place?

Use all the sources of information you can find to determine what your evaluation criteria should be. Take another look at your customer interview notes. Review your charter. Talk to customers, managers, or other interested stakeholders.

Believe it or not, that's not all you must do to prepare your presentation properly. Before you present any ideas as recommendations, don't forget to make sure they will work in your organization. Here are a few issues you may want to consider in this regard:

- What technical limitations must be considered?

- Are there certain elements, such as physical security, that any solution must include?

- What financial constraints must be considered?

- Are any "sacred cows" involved? For example, if your organization has just completed lengthy negotiations with a new vendor, you may want to avoid recommendations that require renegotiation of that agreement.

- Do adequate systems exist to support your recommendations?

- How will the potential improvement be accepted by your organization's culture? Will people accept the new approach? *Don't underestimate the importance of this issue.*

Evaluation Tools

Now that you're ready to fully evaluate your ideas, don't fall into the trap of constantly comparing one idea with another. Evaluate each idea on its own merits. Don't overlook a small improvement that's cheap and easily implemented just because your first priority is a "big hitter." Here are three tools you can use to help evaluate your ideas more effectively:

- *Force field analysis.* This tool, shown on page 120 (figure 6-12), will help your team identify the strengths and weaknesses of your ideas. It also forces the team to think of ways to eliminate weaknesses of ideas while reinforcing their strengths. In fact, force field analysis can be used both to evaluate ideas and to make them better. For more information on this tool, consult pages 195-197 of the Toolbox.

- *Cost-benefit analysis.* This common evaluation tool simply calculates the known or estimated cost of your recommendations, lists all of their tangible and intangible benefits, and compares the two. Cost-benefit analysis normally includes an estimate of the time required for benefits to equal the cost of implementing the change.

- *Review board.* This favorite CIA tool helps to promote critical analysis of ideas. It essentially involves selecting a special group of individuals to provide feedback on ideas before they're presented as recommendations. If you pick the right people and provide the board with good questions, you can receive valuable feedback that can help you improve your idea. For more detailed instructions on how to pick a review board, see pages 218-220 of the Toolbox.

Ranking Tools

Teams often choose to present their recommendations in order of importance. Some teams, however, prefer to specify those recommendations for which team support is very strong. When you need to sort and rank a lot of ideas, you can use the ranking tools we introduced in Chapter III. Recall that:

- *Multi-voting* is a "process of elimination" tool that helps teams turn large lists of ideas into smaller lists of preferred ideas. See page 206 of the Toolbox for more information.

- *Pairwise-ranking* is a technique that assists teams in reaching consensus on how to order ideas by comparing them to each other and determining preferences for each comparison. See pages 211-212 of the Toolbox for more information.

Key Action 5: Present Recommendations

Once you complete your improvement planning efforts, your team will probably present its final recommendations to management. This presentation can take the form of a formal or informal briefing, a written report, or both. Making this presentation is generally the last official responsibility of the team.

Presenting Your Solutions

Your team will probably not want to prepare detailed implementation plans until management accepts your recommendations. What's more, the amount of planning required for any of your recommendations will depend on the complexity, cost, and number of people affected by them. Nonetheless, some preliminary implementation guidelines are necessary to help management evaluate each recommendation you make. Here are some items you may wish to include in your final report:

- A prioritized list of recommendations.

- An explanation of the cost and benefits of each recommendation.

- A list or discussion of issues related to start-up. The team should know if recommendations can be implemented immediately or if they must be phased in or pilot-tested first.

- A list or discussion of implementation-related issues. Will equipment purchases be required? Will people need to be trained? Will new policies have to be issued? Will forms have to be redesigned?

- Documentation that supports the team's findings, conclusions, and recommendations. Include (as one or more appendices) the tree diagrams, Pareto charts, scatter diagrams, flow- charts, etc., that your team developed to settle on the recommendations you're presenting.

- Implementation plan. How will your proposed changes be monitored? Remember that the things you measured to establish a performance baseline are the same things you want to measure after implementing improvements. How will data be collected? Who will be responsible for collecting it? When should data collection begin? How long should this procedure last?

- A discussion of where follow-on efforts might be launched.

Remember that management's view of things may be different than yours. While there is no way to know everything that causes this, keep in mind that scheduling and budgeting issues are almost certainly involved.

Presentation Tools

To help managers evaluate your recommendations and successfully implement them, here are two tools you can use:

- *Gantt chart.* There are many variations of this planning tool, but your team can use it to clarify the relationship between specific implementation tasks, key milestones, and time. For more information, see pages 198-199 of the Toolbox.

- *Action plan.* This is a simple tool that also has many variations. It can help you translate an idea into action by clarifying issues such as: what steps need to be taken, in what sequence, at what time, and on who's watch? The criteria for measuring the completion of each step also may appear in an action plan. For more information, see page 154 of the Toolbox.

Getting Your Solutions Accepted

Management's view of things is no better or worse than yours, but it is different. While there is no way to know everything that causes this difference in perspective, keep in mind that scheduling, budgeting, and other issues are almost certainly involved.

Don't sell yourselves short by failing to consider the criteria management may use to evaluate your findings. Chances are they'll be looking at the following:

- *Your methods.* Management will probably be interested to see if your team followed the right methods in doing your work. They'll also want to know if you used the appropriate tools and procedures to get the job done.

- *Your findings and conclusions.* Of course, managers will want to be sure that you collected the right data and analyzed it properly. They'll also want to determine that the data you've collected support your conclusions about the nature of the issue addressed, root causes, and other factors.

- *Your recommendations.* Managers will certainly consider whether your recommendations are justified by the data you presented. They'll also want to know whether you addressed the level of risk involved in carrying out your recommendations.

Note that these issues are about the way you developed your ideas, not the recommendations themselves. If managers agree with how you carried out the process so far, they will be more willing to accept the results of your work.

Now that you have a better idea of what management will want to know, here are some suggestions for strengthening your case, not only with management, but also with other members of your organization:

- Be prepared to explain how the solution will fit into your organization, as well as who will be affected and how.

- Communicate with all parties who may be affected by your recommendation. Allow them to review your implementation plan. Solicit feedback.

- Make sure everyone understands why the solution is needed. Be prepared to sell your recommendations.

Remember, your goal is to present solutions that will work and be accepted. Even though your team has completed a systematic approach to problem-solving that leads logically to your conclusions and recommendations, other key players in the organization will not be as familiar with your position as you are. Be sure that you've already minimized their potential objections to the changes you're preparing by keeping them updated on the progress of your work.

In any case, though, it's important that you now make an additional effort to share your new understanding with others who must live with your recommendations. Neutralize resistance and you'll improve your prospects for success.

Recommending Prevention: Ongoing Process Monitoring

Most of this chapter has focused on improving performance in ways that will enhance productivity, customer satisfaction, profitability, or other key organizational goals. That's fine, because in all likelihood, your team was chartered to do just that. But you may also be able to recommend ways to better monitor performance on a continuous basis, long after current problems have been solved.

How? Well, as you made an effort to fully understand your process, you may have looked at the process in ways that no one in your organization has before. You also may have identified areas of performance (output characteristics) and measures for which no one routinely collects data. In fact, teams often find that the right things haven't been measured because owners and operators haven't understood the causal link between customer satisfaction and the performance of a specific process.

Teams often find that the right things haven't been measured because owners and operators haven't understood the causal link between customer satisfaction and process performance.

Get the most our of the knowledge you've gained from following the steps outlined in Chapter IV. Review existing process measures and compare them to the ones your team has just developed. Don't hesitate to recommend changes to existing measurement — practices such as the elimination of time-consuming data collection procedures that add little value to the process, or the addition of critical performance-tracking measures that more effectively monitor process performance.

When the right things are measured and monitored on a continuing basis — and this is sometimes the most appropriate use of control charts — operators of a process can see problems as they arise and make corrections before things get out of hand. Through efforts like these, everyone involved can truly gain control of the process.

Tips for a Successful Presentation

- Keep it short and simple.

- Prepare and distribute an agenda. Allow for feedback and modify the agenda if necessary, then stick to it.

- If a draft written report is available, distribute it to attendees in advance.

- Use visual aids such as flipcharts and overhead transparencies. They can focus the discussion and help ensure that all key points are covered.

- Overhead transparencies should use large type and contain few words. Be prepared to elaborate, but don't try to get every point you're making on the transparency.

- Use numbers and facts as much as possible.

- Prepare the room in advance. Is the equipment working? Do you have spare bulbs for the projectors you're using? Enough chairs? Enough handouts?

- Practice beforehand. Rehearsing will help you overcome any nervousness and improve the quality of your presentation.

- Tailor your presentation to your audience. Know who will be there. If at all possible, learn about their attitudes, biases, and knowledge of the subject beforehand.

- Involve your audience. Establish a rapport with them and field their questions.

- Use a flipchart to capture ideas from your audience, including their comments, concerns, and recommendations.

- Don't read directly from your transparencies, other visual aids, or draft report. Talk to the audience and maintain eye contact as much as possible.

- Don't demand an immediate response from management. Managers may need to do some research, themselves, before they can give you an answer.

- Schedule another meeting to discuss report recommendations.

You probably won't be surprised to learn that teams generally feel an immense amount of pride and relief once they've made their presentations. Take some time to enjoy the sense of accomplishment you deserve to feel. In fact, one of the best things everyone involved can do for your organization is to encourage you to hold a final team meeting to discuss the lessons you learned from your improvement effort. Focus this discussion on tools, methods, sources of data, and the problems you encountered. Let everyone involved know what you find out, so that all can share from your experience.

Keep in mind, however, that the improvement process is far from over. Some of you will be participating directly in the upcoming Do-Check-Act phases of the improvement cycle, some of you may not. In any case, we want you to be aware of how your efforts will affect the way your organization conducts its business from now on. That's what the next chapter is all about.

After making your presentation, take some time to enjoy the sense of accomplishment you deserve to feel.

Chapter 7

FROM RECOMMENDATION TO REALITY:

*THE DO-CHECK-ACT
PHASES OF THE PDCA
CYCLE*

So far, this book has deliberately sought to speak personally to you and the members of your team about the challenges involved in process improvement. That's because, up until this point, you and your team were primarily responsible for the success of the improvement effort. While that's still true, in the sense that solid planning increases the probability that a project will succeed, there's a good chance that other members of your organization will play significant roles from now on.

The Process Improvement Cycle

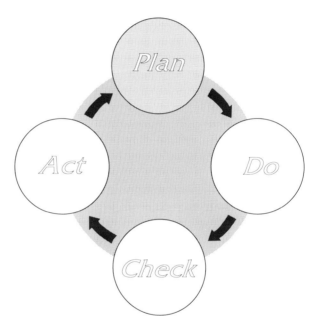

Managers may very well take on the responsibility of directing implementation efforts. If that's the case, much of what you'll soon be reading about will be their concern.

It's also quite possible that members of your team will be called upon to assist them in making your recommendations work. Should that happen, some of you will find yourselves deeply involved in many of the steps outlined here.

Do-Check-Act documents your team's success. It will show the value of your recommendations in dollars or time saved and increased customer satisfaction.

There's also a third possibility — one that's emerged only in the last few years. Some of you may be functioning as self-managed teams that bear the full responsibility for the range of activities that take place during the entire Plan-Do-Check-Act Cycle. If you are a member of such a team, it's likely that you'll be tackling virtually every task we'll be discussing.

Finally, some of you will have completed your work once your team has made its recommendations; you already know that you won't be participating in most of the tasks described in this chapter. No matter. It's still important that you take a look at what's included here.

Why? Because there's nothing more frustrating than launching headlong into a task without knowing how it will all turn out. Read ahead. Find out how the difference you've made will make itself felt throughout your organization. Take pride in a job well done!

A Few Words About Do-Check-Act

As your team made its way through the Plan phase, it figured out how best to improve a process. During the Do and Check phases, you'll discover how well your solutions work and whether or not you and other people in your organization can make them even better. When the Act phase finally arrives, you'll have the satisfaction of seeing your recommendations become part of how your organization does business.

The Do, Check, and Act phases of the PDCA Cycle transform your recommendations into real components of everyday worklife. That transformation can be nearly instantaneous or very gradual; going from Plan to Act can take anywhere from a few days to many months. Small, obvious changes that are supported by everyone and easily put in place can usually be acted upon quickly. In such cases, your organization may implement changes quickly and without a lot of fuss. That's fine, as long as someone takes the time to check the results of your efforts later.

As you know, complex ideas generally take longer to introduce, especially if they cost money or require people to be convinced of their value. During this time, everyone involved can reduce risks of error, gain support for the effort, and maximize the gains those efforts can make by using Do-Check-Act steps to:

- prove that your ideas have value

- look at them from different viewpoints (such as those of managers, co-workers, suppliers, and customers)

- conduct trial runs of improved processes to work the kinks and bugs out of new methods

- calm peoples' fears about new ways of doing things

- ensure that the recommendations are carried out as planned

- get "more bang for the buck" by applying improvements in one process to others

- lay the foundation for future improvements

Finally, Do-Check-Act documents your team's success. Done right, it will show the value of your recommendations in dollars or time saved, increased customer satisfaction, more sales, fewer defects, and other benefits.

DO: Implementing Your Solutions

It's easy to think of the Do phase of the PDCA Cycle as the straightforward, step-by-step implementation of each of the recommendations that management has just approved. Well, it is — and it isn't.

Implementing well-planned recommendations does imply that the hard part is history — that all you need to do now is simply check off each item on a "To Do" list as you complete it. But that's just not true. The challenge of the Do phase really lies in your organization's ability to muster the energy and brainpower it takes to properly manage the implementation.

With proper management, your improved process might even outperform expectations.

This point can't be emphasized enough. Without proper management, your recommendations probably won't materialize in a timely and cost-effective way — you won't be able to observe the gain you've worked so hard to achieve. With proper management, however, your improved process might even outperform expectations.

It probably comes as no surprise to you that there are a good number of tasks that need to be accomplished during the Do phase. The following three key actions, however, summarize what everyone involved will be focusing on. During the Do phase, you must:

- define what must be done

- schedule what must be done

- control what is done

Key Action 1: Define What Must Be Done

By this time, the team veterans among you are well aware of what's involved in defining what you're going to do. In this case, those involved will be identifying the activities that must occur before and after recommendations are implemented.

Should the improvement require the purchase of a new machine, for example, you'd not only have to know that you need to purchase the machine, remove the old one, and install the new one, you'd also have to discern — step by step — what other kinds of activities need to take place to get this done. In this case, whoever's responsible for getting the machine operational needs to know that installing a new machine might require reconfiguring the room it will be placed in, as well as some electrical and plumbing work.

Using Tools and Analysis to Define Implementation Tasks

There are many ways to indicate what specific tasks need to be done in what order. For these purposes, a top-down flowchart is recommended to help you define exactly what needs to happen during this time. First introduced in Chapter III, the top-down flowchart allows you to view the process flow and represent the activities that need to take place in a logical and easily understandable sequence. For more information on constructing and using this tool, please turn to pages 228-229 of the Toolbox.

In preparation for your presentation to management, your team may have done a preliminary estimate of the time, cost, and resources that your recommendations require. Now that at least some of those recommendations have been approved, people will be developing firmer estimates (based on your previous work) of what it will take to implement the change on a trial basis.

Key Action 2: Schedule What Must Be Done

Projects can survive, thrive, or die in relation to how smoothly they are carried out. Implementation schedules are the backbone of an implementation effort. Without adequate scheduling, the most promising projects can flounder and even fall apart completely. The Gantt chart discussed in Chapter VI (and described on pages 198-199 of the Toolbox) can focus all those involved on what, where, and when implementation-related tasks need to be accomplished.

Knowing the above information will set the stage for the upcoming implementation, but such information won't tell you quite enough about how feasible the schedule is. Allocating an appropriate amount of resources to each task, therefore, is a necessary and challenging part of the scheduling process.

It's vital to estimate the amount of work that will be involved in a task and the amount of time it will take a certain number of people and certain types of equipment to complete it. Those involved in scheduling soon learn that they must allow for employee schedule conflicts, illness, equipment downtime, and the potential cost in time and dollars of such important factors. In the likely event that such adjustments to the schedule will need to be made, it's best to build some flexibility into it.

> Projects can survive, thrive, or die in relation to how smoothly they are carried out.

Figure 7-1
Implementation Tracking Chart

Responsibility Code	Task Status Code	Implementation Assignments						Implementation Status					
		JOHN	STEVE	LOUISE	ED	MARY	JOAN	JANUARY	FEBRUARY	MARCH	APRIL	MAY	JUNE
R Responsible	OS On Schedule												
I Keep informed	D Delayed												
S Support	C Completed												
A Advisor													

TASKS												
1. Develop performance specs	R		S	S	R		C					
2. Secure funding		R					D	C				
3. Complete vendor analysis	R	I		A		S	D	C				
4. Purchase new equipment	R	I		S		A			OS			
5. Install new equipment					R	R				OS		
6. Track performance		I	R	S							OS	OS

Key Action 3: Control What Is Done

In order to become and remain successful, an improvement effort must be managed with a firm hand or hands that monitor and consistently track the progress of the project. There are numerous, and more elaborate, systems for doing this, but a chart such as the one shown on this page (figure 7-1) can indicate who is doing what and if he or she is on track, finished, or behind schedule.

Managing the project also demands that those involved evaluate and adjust the implementation schedule as necessary — sometimes even before the need to do so becomes immediately apparent. This activity has already been foreshadowed in **Key Action 2**, but the trick here is to combine and compare the information you've been gathering during your monitoring efforts with the projections you made before the change was implemented.

If certain activities take substantially longer than was predicted, someone will have to figure out what implications this may have for the schedule — and there are always emergencies. At this stage, you won't be simply anticipating emergencies, as you did in **Key Action 2**. There's a chance that someone will have to react quickly to one — for example, a mainframe disaster, and adjust the schedule accordingly.

Managing the Impact of Change on Others

Another aspect of controlling what's done involves not *controlling* people, but *helping* them to manage the changes that occur. As your organization prepares and carries out an implementation plan for the change that's about to be made, some members of your team will probably be helping people to use the new system. This is where the payoff for all of your work begins.

As you know, some changes are quite simple and don't require a formal planning approach. However, the introduction of more complex changes that require operators to change the way they work will also be necessary. Future possibilities, such as applying changes in one process to others, must also be considered.

Implementation Plan

As do the other implementation plans featured in this book, the operator-related implementation plan describes how your solution will actually work. In most cases, this can be a very brief document in outline form. In fact, if you included this as part of your initial presentation to management, you may need to revise it very little at this stage.

In some instances, you'll want to spend more time preparing the plan. This occurs when the change is complicated or expensive, or when there is a high risk of severe problems if the change is not carried out carefully. In addition, if many people in several different processes must change their way of working, your team may want to plan how you'll control variation.

Short or long, the plan must spell out:

- *What will be done during the transition period.* This is a description of the change you're making in the process. Be sure to say what you did before and what you will do now.

- *Expected benefit.* This is a short list of the reasons for making the change.

- *Who will be responsible.* Who will carry out various aspects of the change from old to new procedures? This includes both those who will introduce the change and those who will use it.

> As your organization implements your recommendations, some members of your team will probably be helping people to use the new system.

- *How you will make the change.* This includes preliminary training, notifying other processes, and installing the measurement system.

- *Where the changes will take place.* Which work unit locations will be affected?

- *When the conversion will take place.* You may need to show a schedule for this; if so, consider using a Gantt chart, as described in Chapter VI.

- *The new measurement plan.* Attach a copy for all those involved.

- *The budget for the conversion (if any).*

- *Methods that should be used to monitor the change.*

A good plan, no matter how brief, will show an outsider what you intend to do, by when, and the reason for the change. This way, there will be little or no confusion about the new system.

CHECK: *Determining the Value of Your Recommended Improvements*

During the Check phase of the improvement cycle, your organization will set out to confirm the value of your team's ideas and perhaps improve on them a bit. This will involve a measurement plan, final cost-benefit analysis, and communication with your co-workers, suppliers, and customers.

If your recommendations call for major changes or expensive equipment, it's likely that a number of people will be involved in the tasks outlined below. Performing these tasks will provide the information and experience needed to perfect your solution and show others how to use it. There's another bonus attached to doing this: It will help to convince your co-workers and managers to make the extra effort needed to change the process.

If the change is simple, everyone agrees with it, and management decides to make it without further debate, it won't be necessary to do all the detailed activities listed here. But you do need to measure results. Even if they are minor, such results:

- are valuable to sales people, planners, and price estimators when calculating how long and how much it takes to respond to customer orders

- show that process improvement works

Those who participate in the Check phase will be concerned with two key activities. Those activities will require you to:

- verify the improved performance of your process

- confirm the costs and benefits of improving your process

Key Action 1: Verify the Improved Performance of Your Process

By this point, your organization will be ready to analyze the data collected during the Do phase and find out if things did, in fact, get better as a result of your team's efforts. If so, you'll usually get the go-ahead for a permanent change. If little or no improvement has happened, however, you may have to modify and repeat the pilot projects set up to test your recommendations, or repeat some parts of the Plan phase to develop new solutions. (Usually, you'd return to the activities included in Chapter VI.)

The Measurement Plan

Part of the Check phase is devoted to analyzing the hard data on process performance gathered during the Do phase. A good measurement plan will guide people in doing this. As you know, much of that plan will have been written as you prepare to measure process performance (see Chapter IV). The Check phase will consist mostly of following those directions.

What should you measure? During Do-Check, your co-workers will spend much of their time measuring key aspects of the process or

During the Check phase of the improvement cycle, your organization will set out to confirm the value of your team's ideas and perhaps improve on them.

the root causes of their variation. However, you'll need data on how your solution affected performance and customer satisfaction. If you have all three sets of data, you'll be able to see:

- if improvements in key aspects of the process appear to cause improvement in performance

- if that better performance causes higher customer satisfaction

If so, then you can be much more confident of the link between your solutions and increased customer satisfaction.

It's also best to share the measurement plan with people who will be affected by the changes made. Having everyone agree with the measurements used is essential, so that no one can complain later that your team didn't measure the right things.

A good measurement plan remains your best bet for success in the Check phase. It will keep everyone on course during the weeks or months of the Do phase, so that those involved will have the right data when it comes time to prove the value of your ideas.

Preparing for Permanent Solutions

The measurement plan also gives everyone a chance to try out the performance measurement system that will be put into place during the Act phase. Therefore, management and others will also be thinking not only about measuring key aspects of the process, as they do during the Check phase, but also about what should be measured over the long term in order to keep track of variation and performance in the new system. Here's what they'll be considering:

- The key variables that process operators and managers need to get feedback on during normal operations. Most of the time, these will be fewer in number than those you use during the Check phase. It's most likely that the way they're collected will be given special attention during the Do-Check phases of the improvement effort.

- The sampling and data collection methods that will be used during normal operations in the Act phase. Usually, these will be simpler than those used during Check phase — as your new system becomes stable, your sampling efforts are likely to become smaller and less frequent.

If you're directly involved in these stages of the improvement effort, try to test your ideas about these ongoing measurements during the Do and Check phases. This will save you a lot of time during the Act phase and ensure that decisions made later are guided by good data.

Looking at Results

During the Check phase, those involved will need to verify two things: that tasks were actually done differently and that the changes produced a positive result.

Did things go as planned? Before you begin data analysis, make sure people followed the new procedures.

The same goes for collecting data. In the Plan phase, your team probably did all data collection. But in the Do phase, as mentioned above, other co-workers may handle all or part of the task. They may not be as well trained in data collection, and they probably aren't as motivated as you are to see that the job is done correctly. And there's another factor to take into account: Since Do-Check measurement sometimes goes on for months, people may get tired of it.

Remedies for these problems include training in the new procedures, impressing people with the importance of their role, and periodic checks to make sure they are doing things as planned. As always, ask for their suggestions on how to do this task better.

Did things improve? During the Check phase, those assigned to analyze data will be doing so, according to your measurement plan. They'll be looking for two things:

- the amount of improvement between the baseline period and the end of the measurement period

- whether improvements in process factors and root causes can be linked to improvements in other areas

The focus should be on trends in the data collected. You and others will want to know if performance is trending upward, downward, or staying the same. Don't underestimate the importance of this data. Trend information is always more valuable than simple snapshots of "before" and "after" situations.

Can process improvement be linked to customer satisfaction? It's often tough to show how a single improvement affects customers. However, all you will need to be concerned with is that the improvement affects process performance. Then, if your process's performance goes up and so does customer satisfaction, everyone can be reasonably sure that the improvement you recommended was one of the reasons.

Compare trends. In this part of analysis, those involved will be looking for correlations in the trends affecting key aspects of the process, performance, and customer satisfaction. Here are some hints for looking at these relationships:

- Make a chart that shows changes in performance before and during the Do phase. Those charts can then be compared to see if they trend in the same way.

- An improvement in performance will be less pronounced than that of the aspect of the process involved. This is because performance is affected by many aspects of the process, not just the one you are working on. Likewise, a change in customer satisfaction may not be as striking as an improvement in performance.

Key Action 2: Confirm the Costs and Benefits of Improving the Process

So much for the benefits. Now, how about the costs? Those involved may want to repeat the cost-benefit analysis you did during the Plan phase, using the better information on costs gathered during the Do phase.

Charting the Costs and Benefits of Process Improvement

Estimating Costs

During this phase, you might find that people need more or less time and material than your team originally planned in order to operate the new system. Based on their experience, cost estimates will probably need to be revised.

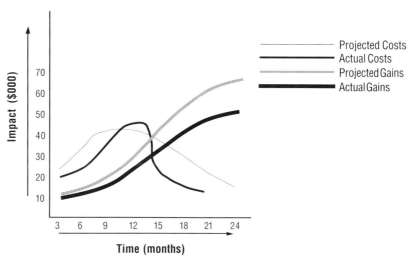

Two types of costs will be looked at:

- *One-time costs.* These include costs for new equipment and facilities needed for the change, including the costs of any new measurement system you plan to install. It also may include the cost of training people to use the new system.

- *Ongoing costs.* These are any labor, supply, or other operating costs over and above existing operating costs.

Estimating Benefits

Management will often find that the benefits resulting from your recommendations have exceeded your original estimate. This information needs to be included in revised cost-benefit calculations.

Ask customers if they've noticed any difference in the service or products they've received. Often they have, and they'll give you positive feedback.

Qualitative Results

Numbers are not everything. How people have reacted to the change is important. Before a new system becomes permanent, everyone will also want to learn about any side effects it may have.

Ask customers if they've noticed any difference in the service or products they've received as a result of your team's improvement. Often they have, and they'll give you positive feedback. Along with hard data, this is the final evidence management needs in order to see the benefit of adopting your ideas. When you get the chance, don't forget to ask them for further suggestions.

Whether or not you're deeply involved in the Check phase, spend a good deal of time talking with co-workers who used the change during the Do phase. Find out what their reaction was to the change. Did they encounter any specific problems? Did they develop solutions for them?

The fact that you asked for their feedback means your co-workers will probably show even more support for your new ideas during the Act phase of the improvement effort. If you continue to treat them as partners in the effort, they will be your best advocates later on.

ACT: Holding the Gain

During the Do and Check phases of the PDCA Cycle, your organization implemented your team's recommendations for improvement and verified the impact they actually made on the process you targeted. At this point, the objective is to hold on to the gain — to make sure that the changes you helped to make become an integral part of the way your organization operates. The Act phase consists of two key actions:

- standardize the improvement

- install the improvement in the process

What about continuous improvement — going beyond the gains you just made? That's the subject of the last part of this chapter. In a very real sense, it's the most important part of this book.

Key Action 1: Standardize the Improvement

In the Plan, Do, and Check phases, your team — and many others — developed and implemented improvements to your process. The focus of the Act phase is to include that new system in standard operating procedure (SOP). Being part of SOP ensures that the quality you designed into the process will stay there. If the improvement is not SOP, each person participating in the new system will soon start using it a bit differently. Over time, these little revisions will add up, until no one does things the way you planned. If that were to happen, major swings in performance would soon emerge — and that would probably put the process right back where you found it originally. What a waste!

There are several actions you and/or management can take to make sure your solution is permanent, as well as capable of further improvement. Since someone probably covered most of these things during the Plan, Do, and Check phases, or gathered the information needed for them, this step won't take very long.

Perfecting the Solution

Now's the time to make final improvements and adjustments to the original solution. Whoever is involved in this phase of the improvement effort will need to review the results of the Do and Check phases for ways to get rid of any bugs or kinks left in the new system. Part of this will involve asking everyone who has taken part so far for their suggestions. The new procedures will then reflect the better solution you and everyone else in the process created.

Whoever is in charge should maintain the Do-Check measurement system your team recommended for a few weeks or months after the Act phase. If this approach is adopted, your organization may discover information that will lead to further improvements.

The focus of the Act phase of the improvement cycle is to standardize the improvement your team has made.

Communicating Check Phase Results

Another activity that you can expect to see early on involves communicating the results of implementation efforts. You may or may not be directly concerned with this, but it's a good idea, in any case, to be aware of how it works. As you know, you'll have both internal and external audiences for information on Do and Check phase results. The most emphasis will be placed on letting the operators, managers, and internal customers and suppliers of your process know how it went. They'll most likely hear:

- that the pilot was a success

- about the types of changes that brought about the success

- who participated (This is important, because people will probably want to talk with them.)

- about plans for the Act phase

If the improvements you helped to make had a measurable effect on your external customers' satisfaction, then find out if and how you can send the same information to them. Doing so can further reinforce your partnership with them — and the importance of that can't be underestimated.

Finally, your organization's in-house newsletter knows how everything turned out. If the improvement if something everyone can use, make sure the newsletter provides technical details and a way to contact key people involved.

Removing Barriers

Somewhere along the way, you may have found that your solution would work much better and more quickly if management helped you to remove a few barriers. Let's say, for example, that some old policies or rules have traditionally required a work step or report that your team found to be unnecessary. Most of the time, managers in your organization can remove such barriers. Sometimes, however, they may need permission to do so from headquarters, so the change may take a bit longer. The careful work you did in the Plan, Do, and Check phases becomes very important at this point: Managers will very likely want and need it to prove the need for a policy change.

Key Action 2: Installing the Improvement in the Process

Even a small change in your process can affect many other processes. During the Act phase, all participants will need to double check for this "ripple" effect:

- Make sure the improvement has not somehow caused problems for your internal supplier and customer processes. It could turn out, for example, that your organization's increased performance has strained your supplier's processes to the limit; they may be having a hard time honoring your requests for materials and information. Or, the improvements may be responsible for producing output faster than your customer processes can use it. If this happens, the extra output may be piling up, and that can be costly to store until it's needed. Unintended costs like these can wipe out the savings gained in your own processes.

- People working in such support areas as planning, inventory, facilities management, and quality control need to know that you are doing things differently so they can adjust their work where necessary. The planning department, for example, will want and need to know that you now can produce output much faster. If management has changed working hours to handle surges, office or facilities management people need to know that, and someone needs to think about any extra costs this might involve. Finally, the inspectors in quality control need to find out as soon as possible that you've reduced errors so much that their services are no longer required.

Publicizing the Work of the Team

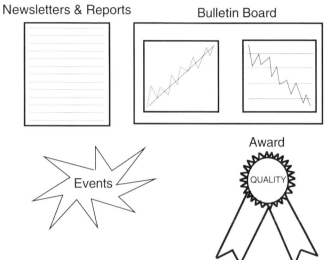

Newsletters & Reports

Bulletin Board

Events

Award

QUALITY

- Check administrative processes, such as personnel, finance, and accounting. If one of your solutions, for example, is to cross-train people in several skills, the personnel department may need to revise job descriptions. And, if your organization employs union members, the labor relations office needs to know about these types of changes, too.

Record the Changes in Operations Manuals

Operations and procedures manuals help ensure that people do things the same way, which reduces variation. They can also offer solutions to routine problems that sometimes appear in a process. Your manuals will need to be updated to include your new system. Whenever you hear about a suggestion for further improvement, suggest that it be recorded in the manual and sent to all process operators.

If your organization doesn't use written procedures, suggest that they do so. Why? Believe it or not, your managers and co-workers will eventually like having a ready reference for procedures, especially when they're training new employees.

Train People in the New Procedures

As you'll recall from the earlier chapters, training is a part of your process, just like people, materials, methods, equipment, and your organization's environment. Many process problems can be traced to poor training, or no training at all — chances are you may have already discovered this.

The amount of training people will need depends on whether the changes you recommended are simple or complex. Training for a simple change might involve sitting around a table and reviewing new written procedures with everyone before trying them out together. More complex changes and those requiring new skills, however, will benefit from a training curriculum, training aids, and structured practice time. Even if members of your team don't conduct this training personally, you'll probably be asked for feedback on it.

Measurement System

Your organization will need to convert the measurement system used during the Do and Check phases into an ongoing, routine way of monitoring performance. In addition, it may adopt some of the process measures your team developed with the help of Chapter IV. Accomplishing this is probably the most important thing your organization can do to hold on to the gains made by your improvement.

There's a chance that someone will complain that measuring performance regularly is too expensive — a waste of time. If and when you hear such objections (and you probably will, if he or she knows you had something to do with the change), ask the person if he or she would fly in an airplane that didn't contain an instrument panel. Explain that process measurements are like gauges on such a panel — they show how critical parts of your process are performing and give early warning of serious problems. Finally, ask him or her to consider what would happen if you didn't measure performance — you would eventually lose what you worked so hard to gain during the process improvement effort!

Above all, do let anyone who complains know that ongoing measurement will not cost nearly as much as it did during the Do and Check phases. You'll want to track a few key factors in the process — just enough to let the right people know how it's performing. What's more, when a process becomes stable, as it will as a result of everyone's efforts, employees will need to take smaller and fewer samples than they did when it was still new and unstable.

Some aspects that those involved will need to consider when planning for ongoing measurement are described below.

Your team's improvement project started with what was important to customers; the ongoing measurement system must maintain this focus. Once you get the go-ahead, continue to collect data on your customers' expectations and satisfaction, as well as the performance results related to these data.

While customers remain the primary focus of your organization's process improvement efforts, the chief purpose of ongoing measurement is to control variation and detect problems early. The system

Many process-related problems can be traced to poor training procedures. A training curriculum, training aids, and structured practice time will help your organization solve this problem.

needs to reveal unwanted variation, recognize potential problems, and point to their possible causes.

The next most important reason for measuring is to improve a process even more over time. This is another reason for continuing to monitor customer expectations and satisfaction, related output characteristics, and key aspects of the process: changes in these factors will point out continuing improvement opportunities.

Remember, too, that it's important for employees to know how to measure the performance of the process. It can't hurt to remind those in charge to be sure that the people who operate the process get the feedback they need to control and improve it.

Finally, there's the issue of what to do about the natural human tendency to neglect ongoing measurement. In the rush of daily work, people will assign a low priority to measurement. Their work will probably get sloppy — they'll forget to record important data, draw samples the wrong way, and sometimes even make up the numbers. Recommend that whoever is in charge of the measurement system regularly check on how employees are measuring data. Such checks must be a part of your measurement system.

Resistance to Change

If you've done everything described thus far, you probably won't find much resistance to change within your own process. This is because the right people were involved in making the change: you and your fellow team members or co-workers, as well as suppliers and customers from whom you sought advice and feedback.

However, management may ask you or other members of your team to help transfer your solution to other processes — and you may encounter resistance when you try. Just in case you find yourself involved in this kind of activity, here are some guidelines that can help to prevent or overcome such resistance:

- *Show respect.* People may tell you all the reasons the "old" way is better – especially if they worked on making it better. Respect this, and indicate that the old way is good. Never say that people are doing something wrong.

- *Listen.* Allow people to ventilate their opinions and feelings about both the old way and the new. Write down their concerns so you can address them later.

- *Explain.* Sometimes people just want to know "why." Be sure to explain the problems and opportunities addressed by the change.

- *Describe* the new way in detail; this helps avoid misunderstanding. It's also best to describe the benefits of the new way in terms that process operators and managers can easily understand.

Addressing Resistance to Change

Reasons Why People Resist Change	Actions to Address Resistance
Loss of Control	Achieve active involvement in process
Uncertaintly	Provide complete information
The "Difference" Effect	Make change manageable
Loss of Face	Put past actions in a positive light
Concerns About Future Competence	Supply adequate training
Ripple Effect: Disruption	Provide flexibility
More Work	Recognize, support, and reward effort
Past Resentments	Bring them into the open and deal with them
Real Threat	Avoid creating "losers" where at all possible

Adapted from Rosabeth Moss Kanter, *The Change Masters: Innovation and Entrepreneurship in the American Corporation,* 1983.

- *Demonstrate the change.* One way to do this is to have people from other processes visit you and see the new system in action. If appropriate, you can make videotapes that show your process's new system in action.

- *Involve others.* Just as you joined a team to develop an improvement, other processes might use teams to introduce it to others. This always increases acceptance because people do not resist change as much as they resist being forced to change. Also, using teams to introduce changes in a process helps ensure that specific factors involved in adjusting the change to fit the requirements of a new location are taken into account.

Leveraging Improvement

Think you've finished yet? Well, yes and no. Yes, your work is probably over if you think it's unlikely that your process can get any better or that it can't be transferred to other processes. No, it's not over if you think that continuously improving your work is important. If so, read on. . .

Look for ways to improve *how* you improve and your company or agency will become a learning organization.

Plan-Do-Check-Act is a Cycle

As your team worked its way through the steps of PDCA, you probably noticed several other opportunities for improvement. These may include the secondary causes of problems, as shown in the Pareto diagrams you developed, or other things. Now is the time to go back and work on them.

The results from this "second-time-around" PDCA Cycle may not loom as large as the first — but you will probably need less time and fewer resources to produce them. This is because you already have the basic background data you need to analyze root causes and form plans. In addition, you and your whole team will have become old hands at process improvement and PDCA by then, so you'll work faster and better.

Even if it is time for your team to take a breather, someone within your organization should continue to pursue the opportunities for improvement you helped to discover. Why? Well, because unless you're improving, you're coasting, and

the only

way to

coast is

downhill.

In short, it's best to always look for *ways to improve how you improve*. Do this, and your company or agency will become a learning organization. Learning organizations always have the best advantages: They can adjust to changes, make new things in new ways, and use every bit of their employees' talent.

And it is *people* who make the difference.

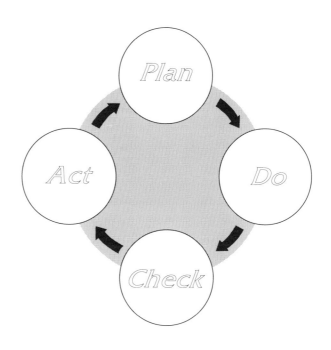

TOOLBOX

Action Plan

Bar Chart

Brainstorming

Cause-and-Effect Diagram

Challenge Assumptions

Checksheets

Control Charts

Deployment Chart

Detailed Flowchart

Force Field Analysis

Gantt Chart

Histogram

Idealized Redesign

Multi-voting

Nominal Group Technique

Opportunity Grid

Pairwise Ranking Matrix

Pareto Diagram

Pie Chart

Review Board

Run Chart

Scatter Diagram

Solution Map

Top-Down Flowchart

Tree Diagram

Problem:_____   *Action Plan*

Improvement Objective:_____

Action Item	Responsible Person/Office	Completion Date	Measureable Criteria

An action plan, as the name suggests, serves as a bridge between an idea and a set of actions required to implement it. An action plan can be simple or detailed, depending on the nature, cost implications, and complexity of your idea. Develop an action plan for implementing your recommendations when you believe that it will:

- help managers understand the feasibility of your idea

- increase the chances of getting your idea accepted

How to Use

1. Identify the key actions required to implement your idea and write them down in sequential order.

2. Determine who should perform each action.

3. For each action, establish criteria for determining that the action has been completed.

Helpful Hints

- To identify who should perform each action, use individual names, position titles, or organizational units, as appropriate

- Detailed action plans may be required once ideas have been accepted. When you're using an action plan to support an idea that has not yet been accepted, however, keep it simple to avoid wasting valuable time.

- You can also include target dates for completion of each step in the plan.

Bar Chart

A bar chart not only orga-
nizes, summarizes, and displays
data so that it can be easily analyzed, it also shows quantities and
the relationships among them
very clearly. The bars in a bar
chart may run either vertically or
horizontally. Solid or broken
lines may be used instead of or in
combination with bars to display
more complicated data.

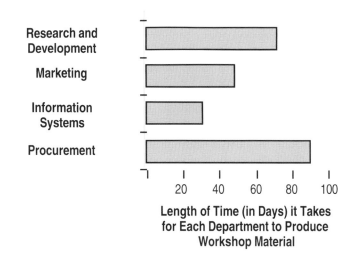

**Length of Time (in Days) it Takes
for Each Department to Produce
Workshop Material**

How to Use

1. Determine what data you want to display and what relationship exists between the data you've chosen.

2. Decide on the unit of measure that will most accurately display your data. For example, if the data value is small, the
   size of the intervals between each scale marking should be
   small. Let's say the largest data point is 100. In that case,
   scale markings should be made in denominations of 10 or denominations of 20, as shown in the illustration on this page.

3. Create the chart after you've determined the scales you're
   going to use on the vertical and horizontal axes and you've
   properly labeled both axes.

4. Finally, determine how to present the bars. Do you want to
   present the bars in sequential order in the illustration, in as-
   cending order (smallest to largest), or in descending order
   (largest to smallest)? Once you've decided how you want
   your bar chart to look, it takes just a few moments to complete it.

Helpful Hints

- To make bar charts easier to read and interpret, omit any un-necessary data from the chart. If necessary, use several charts instead of trying to put too much information on one chart.

Brainstorming

Brainstorming is simply a technique for using the subconscious — the most creative portion of the brain — to generate ideas. Its origins can be traced back at least as far as the 1930s, when it was used by Alex Osborn, an advertising executive. Osborn came up with this technique to circumvent his colleagues' skepticism or resistance to change and thus encourage their ability to think creatively.

The power of brainstorming lies in its ability to bring about what's known as synergy — where the total effect of team efforts is greater than the sum of the individual efforts that each team member could have made on his or her own. Here's how it works: Let's say, for example, that one team member comes up with an idea that is vague or unworkable. Nonetheless, it triggers a thought in another team member's mind. He or she then modifies it, and another team member then builds on the idea further until the team ends up with an innovative idea that no one person could have devised alone.

You can use brainstorming alone or in combination with other tools such as cause-and-effect diagrams and solution maps. Use brainstorming whenever your team wants to create ideas, especially ideas about how to solve problems.

How to Use

1. Define the problem. Often your first attempt at definition will be too broad. Refine it. Make sure everyone shares the same understanding of the problem. Broadly defined problems encourage broad, ill-defined solutions. As a result, team energy is insufficiently focused. Ironically, the wildest flights of fancy come from asking detailed, focused questions.

2. Plan for sessions. Allow time for participants to mull the problem over. Plan a brainstorming session at the end of one meeting and schedule it for the next.

3. Pick the right people. Don't always limit brainstorming sessions to team members, but limit the number of participants

to no more than 12. Invite people who are familiar with the problem. Select people who represent a mixture of professional specialties, backgrounds, and attitudes.

4. Provide outside participants with written invitations. Be sure to give them the question/problem to be brainstormed. Provide them with adequate advance notice (a week is good).

5. Establish ground rules. It is essential that participants suspend judgment during the session. Reinforce a ban on negative thinking.

6. Capture every idea. You don't have to record each one word for word, but you do need to capture the essence of every idea. Ideas that you don't record will probably be lost. Use one or even two full-time recorders so that you can capture every idea without interrupting the flow of the session.

7. Establish a time limit. It's often best to let the group know in advance how long the brainstorming session will last. Try to limit each session to 20 minutes.

8. Work through lulls. Ideas frequently flow for a while and then stop occurring to people as quickly as they did at first. If you can push through these inevitable lulls, you'll be rewarded for your work. Sometimes the best ideas emerge in the latter stages of brainstorming sessions.

9. Organize, categorize, and evaluate. Once the session is completed, organize all the ideas you've collected. Weed out repetitive ideas. Place similar ideas into categories and label each category.

Helpful Hints

- Think of fun ways to discourage judgmental and negative thinking. For example:

  - Ring a bell whenever someone violates your brainstorming ground rules.

  - Provide participants with nerf balls to throw at "idea assassins," people who shoot down ideas as soon as they're offered.

- To help work through lulls, try the following techniques:

  - Save an idea or two for the occasion. When things slow down, throw these ideas out to get the process moving again.

  - Ask your recorders to read back ideas from the existing list to rekindle team energy.

  - Turn the problem upside-down — define it from a different perspective. For example, you might refocus your perception of the problem from "how do we reduce service delivery delays?" to "how do we deliver service to the customer in two days?"

  - Take a five-minute break. Encourage participants to stand up and walk around or think about something else, then resume the session.

  - Determine how many ideas you want to generate during the session. Encourage the team to persist through lulls to reach this goal.

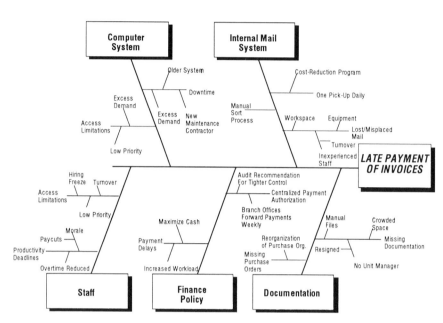

Cause-and-Effect Diagram

The cause-and-effect diagram is one of the most useful basic quality tools. Also known as Ishikawa diagrams (after Dr. Kaoru Ishikawa, the Japanese quality expert who popularized their use in his country) and fishbone diagrams (because a completed diagram can resemble the skeleton of a fish), cause-and-effect diagrams help team members organize information, identify knowledge gaps, and clarify relationships between process factors. They can be used to study just about any issue, and they're easy to use.

While individuals can develop cause-and-effect diagrams, teams produce the most effective ones. An excellent tool to use in a brainstorming session, the cause-and-effect diagram helps team members focus on the issue at hand and immediately sort ideas into useful categories. Like a puzzle, completed cause-and-effect diagrams organize seemingly unrelated pieces of information into a clear, meaningful picture. In short, the diagram helps team members understand why things happen the way they do.

There are two basic approaches to constructing a cause-and-effect diagram. One is called the outside-in approach and the other the inside-out approach. Each shares the same objective of uncovering root causes of your problem — and when completed they look the same. They merely approach the task from different perspectives.

How to Use the Outside-In Approach

1. Determine the effect you want to analyze and state it in a few

words. You could state it as a problem (such as 40 percent of invoices are paid late) or as a quality goal (pay 95 percent of invoices within 30 days). Be sure that all team members agree with the problem statement. This problem statement is the effect you will build on.

2. Generate some ideas about the major causes of the problem. Write down the causes on an angle so they look like branches flowing to the main horizontal branch (see illustration on page 160). You can start with general categories such as people, methods, equipment, environment, etc. Your headings should be broad enough to break down further. If possible, identify more specific major causes, such as internal mail, documentation, finance policy, etc.

3. Brainstorm all the possible causes for each main cause. Organize these ideas in successive levels to reflect the relationship between them. It's okay to repeat "sub-causes" in several places if it makes sense to do so. Keep defining these causes and relating them to each other. At each succeeding level of detail, ask "What causes or contributes to this problem?"

How to Use the Inside-Out Approach

1. Begin with the same first step, as shown above.

2. Next, conduct a brainstorming session to identify as many potential causes as possible. Don't worry about categories or relationships.

3. Edit your list and combine similar ideas into separate categories.

4. Select a label for each category — a word or phrase that accurately summarizes all of the ideas contained in the category. These labels are your major causes.

5. Explore the relationship between the causes listed in each category. Relate them to each other and arrange them in a hierarchy under the major cause you've identified.

Helpful Hints

- Think big when constructing cause-and-effect diagrams. Although you've focused on problems in the process under review, some of the causes of these problems probably lie outside that process. Consider your organization's culture, environment, internal politics, employee-related issues, and external factors as potential sources of problems.

- Get everyone to participate. Each team member brings a unique perspective to the effort and has a unique contribution to make. Generally, a complete picture of any problem exceeds the specific knowledge of any one person. That's why this tool works especially well with teams.

- Quantify the problem and as many of its causes as possible. This will improve the team's understanding of the problem. It will also facilitate your efforts to rank root causes and identify improvement opportunities.

- When the team doesn't know why problems occur, members need to go and find out. Ask questions. Interview key people and collect the data you'll need to understand the problem better.

- When using an inside-out approach, use sticky notes to record individual ideas. Brainstorm individually for a while and have team members literally stick their ideas on the wall. Your team can then gather around the wall of ideas and eliminate redundant ones, rephrase them if necessary, and organize them into separate categories by simply moving them around.

Challenge Assumptions

There are many simple techniques you can use once your team has accepted the need to challenge the status quo continuously, especially during idea generation. The purpose of challenging assumptions is simple — to come up with new and innovative ideas, you need to look at problems from many points of view. To be able to do that as effectively as possible, you need to escape the self-imposed constraints that traditional assumptions about problems often create.

How to Use

There are countless techniques you can use to help the team challenge existing assumptions about your problem. Try some out. Make up some more. Here are some guidelines to get you started:

1. State your problem.

2. Write down as many existing assumptions about the problem as you can think of.

3. Try reversing the assumption. Transform it into the opposite of what it is now. If you currently assume, for example, that approval from a department head is required for all transactions, assume that such approval will no longer be required.

4. Try modifying the assumptions. Revise each assumption to make it better or easier to deal with. Change a name, time frame, location, etc. For example, assume that supervisors, rather than department heads, need to approve transactions.

5. Try viewing your assumptions from the perspective of another person, work group, or organization. Suppose your assumption is that it takes a maximum of three days to move requisitions through your internal mail system. What would Federal Express say about that assumption?

Helpful Hints

- If your team identifies many existing assumptions about your problem, select the three or so that are most significant and focus on them.

- When your challenging efforts create a spark and lively discussions follow, it sometimes makes sense to conduct a formal brainstorming session based on your new perspective.

- Remember to write your ideas down.

Checksheets

A checksheet simply provides you with a predesigned format for recording data. Using checksheets makes data collection easier, since those who use them to gather data merely have to make checkmarks in the correct places. This not only reduces the possibility of human error, it also provides

Wasteful Energy Habits	week			
	1	2	3	Total
Long showers	III	I	II	6
Lights left on	IIII	III	IIII	11
Windows left open	II	I		3
AC set below 72°	I	II	II	5
Door left open	IIII	IIII	III	13
Total	15	12	11	38

a common standard for data collection so that everyone involved collects data in the same way. (Otherwise, the data could be useless.)

There are many ways to make a checksheet. Here are some guidelines to help your team design checksheets that are simple, clear, and complete.

How to Use

1. Be sure you fully understand the purpose for data collection before designing a checksheet. What information do you need? What are you investigating?

2. Make the instructions clear. It should be easy to figure out what should and should not go into each check-off block. This can't be emphasized enough. If your checksheet isn't clear, each data collector will fill out the checksheet differently, and your data will be unusable.

3. When it's necessary to distinguish between different categories of data, make sure the checksheet clearly shows data collectors what to do. For example, the checksheet shown on this page categorizes or stratifies data according to individual lot numbers. Depending on your process, it may be necessary to stratify data by the individual workers involved, machines that are used, shift, time of day, date, product, etc.

4. Use a picture. If you are collecting data about errors on requisition forms or vouchers, have the data collector make checks right on a copy of the appropriate form. This will not only allow you to see how many errors occur, but where they occur most frequently. If you are screening incoming material for damage or defects, have the data collector indicate where defects are located by making checks on a picture of the item.

5. Verify that the checksheet is accurate and complete. Be sure that everything you want to check is indicated on it.

6. Make sure that checksheets are user-friendly. Often, this means listing items on the checksheet in the order they will be encountered.

Helpful Hints

- Don't try to put too much on one checksheet. Remember, it's a tool to simplify data collection.

- Use separate checksheets when necessary. By using more than one checksheet to measure a complicated process, you'll be able to collect essential data without sacrificing simplicity.

Control Charts

X̄ and R Control Chart

The X̄ and R chart is the right control chart to use when you collect samples of variable data. An X̄ and R chart is actually two charts — a range (R) chart measures short-term variation and an averages (X̄) chart measures long-term variation.

Sampling Table

	Process Rate (items/hr.)	Erratic	Stable
Sample Frequency:	Under 10	8 hours	8 hours
	10-19	4 hours	8 hours
	20-49	2 hours	4 hours
	50-100	1 hour	2 hours
	Over 100	1/2 hour	1 hour
Sample Size:		5-10	4-6
Sample Method:		Random	Consecutive or Random

The example above is provided to illustrate each step in the How to Use section below and make the instructions easier to follow and understand. A completed control chart based on the example is also provided on page 173.

Let's use the same invoice payment team discussed throughout this book. For this particular example, assume that the team has focused on the time required to process invoices for payment. They've determined that approximately 50 invoices are processed each day.

Since measuring them all would be too time-consuming, team members decided to use samples. They used a sampling table to select a sample size of five invoices per day, chosen at random. Their results are shown in the following table:

How to Use

1. You will analyze the ranges (R) chart first and the sample averages (X̄) chart second.

2. Compute R for each subgroup by subtracting the smallest value from the largest value. For example, R for subgroup 1 is equal to 11.2 – 9.4, or 1.8. R for all 20 subgroups is shown on the control chart on page 173.

3. Scale the range portion (the lower portion) of the chart so that all of the R values computed in step 2 can be plotted.

Invoice Payment Samples

Subgroup	Individual Readings
1	11.1, 9.4, 11.2, 10.4, 10.1
2	9.6, 10.8, 10.1, 10.8, 11.0
3	9.7, 10.0, 10.0, 9.8, 10.4
4	10.1, 8.4, 10.2, 9.4, 11.0
5	12.4, 10.1, 10.7, 10.1, 11.3
6	10.1, 10.2, 10.2, 11.2, 10.1
7	11.0, 11.5, 11.8, 11.0, 11.3
8	11.2, 10.0, 10.9, 11.2, 11.0
9	10.6, 10.4, 10.5, 10.5, 10.9
10	8.3, 10.2, 9.8, 9.5, 9.8
11	10.6, 9.9, 10.7, 10.2, 11.4
12	10.8, 10.2, 10.5, 8.5, 9.9
13	10.7, 10.7, 10.8, 8.6, 11.4
14	11.3, 11.4, 10.4, 10.6, 11.1
15	11.4, 11.2, 11.4, 10.1, 11.6
16	10.1, 10.1, 9.7, 9.8, 10.5
17	10.7, 12.8, 11.2, 11.2, 11.3
18	11.9, 11.9, 11.6, 12.4, 11.4
19	10.8, 12.1, 11.8, 9.4, 11.6
20	12.4, 11.1, 10.8, 11.0, 11.9

4. Plot the points computed in step 2 (the R values) on the range portion (lower portion) of the control chart.

5. Compute $\overline{R}$, which is the average of all the range values computed in step 2. In the example:

$$\overline{R} = (R_1 + R_2 + R_3 ... R_{20})/20 = 1.59$$

6. Using the table below, which was developed by the American Society for Quality Control to avoid having to use complicated formulas for computing control limits, select A_2, D_3, and D_4 based upon the subgroup size of the data you collected. Subgroup size refers to the number of data points in each data collection group. For example, if you collected five data points on Monday and five more on each of the following days, the subgroup size would be five.

$\overline{X}$ and R Chart Table

subgroup size	A_2	D_3	D_4	subgroup size	A_2	D_3	D_4
2	1.880	0	3.268	6	0.483	0	2.004
3	1.023	0	2.574	7	0.419	0.076	1.924
4	0.729	0	2.282	8	0.373	0.136	1.864
5	0.577	0	2.114	9	0.337	0.184	1.816
				10	0.308	0.223	1.777

7. Compute the upper control limit for the range chart (UCL_R) by multiplying D_4 times the $\overline{R}$.

$$UCL_R = D_4 \times \overline{R} = 2.114 \times 1.59 = 3.36$$

8. Compute the lower control limit for the range chart (LCL_R) by multiplying D_3 times $\overline{R}$. (For subgroup sizes of six or smaller, note that D_3 equals zero. Therefore, the LCL_R for subgroup sizes six or smaller will always be zero because zero times any number is zero.)

$$LCL_R = D_3 \times \overline{R} = 0 \times 1.59 = 0$$

9. Draw the control lines computed in steps 7 and 8 on the range portion of the control chart (lower portion).

If any of the plotted points exceed either of the control lines, and if you know why this occurred (that is, you are able to identify the special cause of this abnormal variation), remove the identified point from the data set and recompute and plot the data using steps 2 through 9 above. If you don't know the special causes associated with the point(s) that is/are out of control, conduct further investigations. If you still can't find the special cause(s), leave the points as they are.

10. Compute $\overline{X}$ for each subgroup by adding all of the values in a subgroup together and dividing the sum by the number of values in the subgroup.

    For example, $\overline{X}$ for subgroup 1 is equal to

    $$\frac{11.1 + 9.4 + 11.2 + 10.4 + 10.1}{5} = 10.44$$

    $\overline{X}$ for all 20 subgroups is shown in the control chart on page 173.

11. Scale the $\overline{X}$ portion (the upper portion) of the chart so that all the $\overline{X}$ values computed in step 10 can be plotted.

12. Compute $\overline{\overline{X}}$, which is the average of all the subgroup averages and is called the grand average. In our example:

    $$\overline{\overline{X}} = (\overline{X}_1 + \overline{X}_2 + \overline{X}_3 \ldots + \overline{X}_{20})/20 = 10.66$$

13. Compute the upper control limit for the $\overline{X}$ chart by multiplying A_2 times $\overline{R}$ and then adding $\overline{\overline{X}}$.

    $$\text{UCL } \overline{X} = \overline{\overline{X}} + (A_2 \times \overline{R}) = 10.66 + (.577 \times 1.59) = 11.58$$

14. Compute the lower control limit for the $\overline{X}$ chart by multiplying A_2 times $\overline{R}$ and then subtracting this from $\overline{\overline{X}}$.

    $$\text{LCL } \overline{X} = \overline{\overline{X}} - (A_2 \times \overline{R}) = 10.66 - (.577 \times 1.59) = 9.74$$

15. Enter the upper and lower control lines for $\overline{X}$ on the control chart.

If any of the plotted points exceed either of the control lines, and if you know why this occurred (that is, you are able to identify the special cause of this abnormal variation), remove the identified point from the data set and recompute and plot the data using steps 10 through 15 above. If you don't know the special causes associated with the point(s) that is/are out of control, conduct further investigations. If you still can't find the special cause(s), leave the points as they are.

Helpful Hints

- When collecting data that will be plotted on a control chart, use the same subgroup size each time data are collected — that is, if you take five samples on day one, take five on all subsequent days. This will allow you to use the computation tables provided with the control chart instructions rather than having to calculate the data using time-consuming statistical methods.

Note

After you've read through the instructions and have walked through the example on page 173, you'll probably be wondering what the team should do with the information it has collected. Since the X chart shows that the process is out of control in several places, the team's next step would be to investigate the points that are out of control (for example, the invoices that took an especially long or short time to process) to find out what caused them to take the amount of time they did.

Doing so would be very helpful here because one of the points is out of control on the "good side." Finding causes for this unexpectedly good performance may produce ideas for fundamental process changes that would make it possible for this good performance to occur all the time.

$\overline{X}$ and R Chart Worksheet

1. You will analyze the ranges (R) chart first and the sample averages ($\overline{X}$) chart second.

2. Compute R for each subgroup by subtracting the smallest value from the largest value.

3. Scale the range portion (the lower portion) of the chart so that all of the R values computed in step 2 can be plotted.

4. Plot the points computed in step 2 (the R values) on the range portion (the lower portion) of the control chart.

5. Compute $\overline{R}$, which is the average of all the range values computed in step 2.

    Where k is the number of subgroups.

    $\overline{R} = (R_1 + R_2...R_k)/k = $ _____

6. Using the table on page 168, select A_2, D_3, and D_4 based upon the subgroup size of the data you collected.

7. Compute the upper control limit for the range chart (UCL_R) by multiplying D_4 times the $\overline{R}$.

    $UCL_R = D_4 \times \overline{R} = $ _____

8. Compute the lower control limit for the range chart (LCL_R) by multiplying D_3 times $\overline{R}$.

    $LCL_R = D_3 \times \overline{R} = $ _____

9. Draw the control lines computed in steps 7 and 8 on the range portion of the control chart (lower portion).

10. Compute $\overline{X}$ for each subgroup by adding all of the values in a subgroup together and dividing the sum by the number of values in the subgroup.

11. Scale the $\overline{X}$ portion (the upper portion) of the chart so that all of the $\overline{X}$ values computed in step 10 can be plotted.

12. Compute $\overline{\overline{X}}$, which is the average of all the subgroup averages and is called the grand average.

$$\overline{\overline{X}} = (\overline{X}_1 + \overline{X}_2 + \overline{X}_3 \ldots + \overline{X}_k)/k = \underline{\hspace{3cm}}$$

13. Compute the upper control limit for the $\overline{X}$ chart by multiplying A_2 times $\overline{R}$ and then adding $\overline{\overline{X}}$.

$$UCL_{\overline{X}} = \overline{\overline{X}} + (A_2 \times \overline{R}) = \underline{\hspace{3cm}}$$

14. Compute the lower control limit for the $\overline{X}$ chart by multiplying A_2 times $\overline{R}$ and then subtracting this from $\overline{\overline{X}}$.

$$LCL_{\overline{X}} = \overline{\overline{X}} - (A_2 \times \overline{R}) = \underline{\hspace{3cm}}$$

15. Draw the $UCL_{\overline{X}}$ and $LCL_{\overline{X}}$ on the upper portion of the chart on page 173.

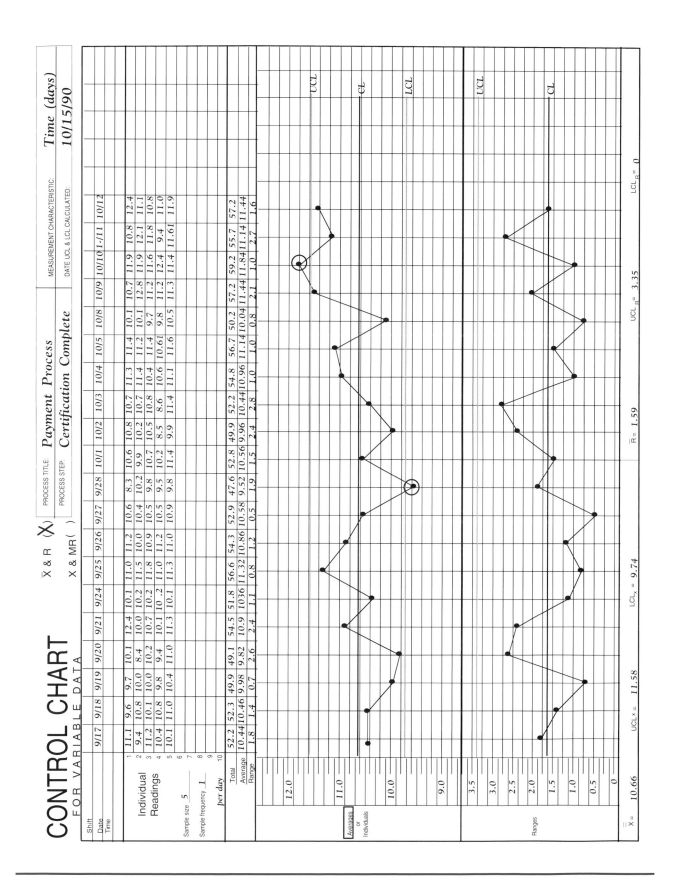

X and MR Table

Subgroup Number	Weekly Overpayments ($)
1	800
2	850
3	740
4	1050
5	930
6	1110
7	1040
8	1040
9	900
10	1000
11	1170
12	1030
13	1620
14	1160
15	1150
16	1100
17	1200
18	1100
19	1020
20	1010
21	1050
22	1030
23	1150
24	1110

X and MR Control Chart

The X and MR chart is the right control chart to use when you're:

- plotting individual values of variable data, instead of samples

- measuring ratios of characteristics

- using samples and the variation within each is very small

The X and MR chart works on the same principle as the $\overline{X}$ and R chart. Since there is no sample range to represent short-term variation, calculate a moving range (MR) (which is simply the difference between any given point and the one before it). There is no MR for the first individual value since there is no preceding point with which to compare it.

There is no need for a table of constants with this chart (as there was with the $\overline{X}$ and R chart), since the subgroup size is always two. The constants are built into the formulas used in the steps below.

Like $\overline{X}$ and R charts, the X portion of the chart represents long-term overall variation. However, the plotted points represent individual variables, not sample averages.

In this case, a team studying the financial system, first referred to on page 88 wanted to measure the dollar value of overpayments on a weekly basis. The financial records had already captured this information, so a single piece of variable data could be plotted for each week. The results of the team's data collection efforts are shown in the table on this page.

The completed control chart on page 177 illustrates control limits for both the MR and X portions of the chart. Note that the MR chart has two points that are out of control. The control limits are added to the X chart to illustrate which individual value is causing the abnormal indication.

As always, the team's action is to investigate the week indicated in an attempt to discover the assignable cause for the unexpectedly high amount of incorrect payments.

Once an assignable cause is discovered, as indicated in steps 6 through 11 below, the out of control point should be removed from the calculations and a new set of control limits computed.

How to Use

1. You'll analyze the moving range (MR) chart first and the individual variables (X) chart second.

2. Compute the moving range MR for each subgroup. Remember there is no MR associated with the first X value.

3. Scale the MR portion of the chart (the lower portion). Remember that the first plotted point should be located at the second position along the time (horizontal) axis because there is no MR for the first point.

4. Compute the average of the MR values (called $\overline{MR}$) by adding all of the MR values and dividing the total by the number of MR values. Keep in mind that the number of MR values will always be one less than the number of X values because there's no MR value for the first X value.

$$\overline{MR} = (MR_1 + MR_2 + ... + MR_{(k-1)})/(k - 1) = 131$$

Where k is the number of subgroups.

5. Compute the moving range upper control limit (UCL_{MR}) by multiplying $\overline{MR}$ times 3.268.

$$UCL_{MR} = 3.268 \times \overline{MR} = 3.268 \times 131 = 428$$

Note: The moving range lower control limit (LCL_{MR}) is always zero.

6. Draw the upper and lower control limits computed in steps 4 and 5 on the MR chart. (Remember that it's the lower chart on the graph paper).

If any of the plotted points exceed either of the control lines, and if you know why this occurred (that is, you are able to identify the special cause of this abnormal variation), remove the identified point from the data set and recompute and plot the data using steps 1 through 6. If you don't know the special causes associated with the point(s) that is/are out of control, conduct further investigations. If you still can't find the special cause(s), leave the points as they are.

7. Scale the vertical axis of the X portion of the control chart (upper portion) and plot the X points.

8. In preparation for computing the upper and lower control limits in steps 9 and 10, compute $\overline{X}$ for all the X values.

$$\overline{X} = (X_1 + X_2 + ... + X_k)/k = 1057$$

9. Compute the upper control limit for X values (UCL_X) using the following formula:

$$UCL_X = \overline{X} + (3 \times [\overline{MR}/1.128]) =$$

$$= 1057 + (3 \times [131/1.128]) = 1405$$

10. Compute the lower control limit for the X values (LCL_X) using the following formula:

$$LCL_X = \overline{X} - (3 \times [\overline{MR}/1.128])$$

$$= 1057 - (3 \times [131/1.128]) = 709$$

11. Draw the upper and lower control limits computed in steps 9 and 10 on the X chart. (Remember that it's the upper chart on the graph paper.)

If any of the plotted points exceed either of the control lines, and if you know why this occurred (that is, you are able to identify the special cause of this abnormal variation), remove the identified point from the data set and recompute and plot the data using steps 7 through 11 above. If you don't know the special causes associated with the point(s) that is/are out of control, conduct further investigations. If you still can't find the special cause(s), leave the points as they are.

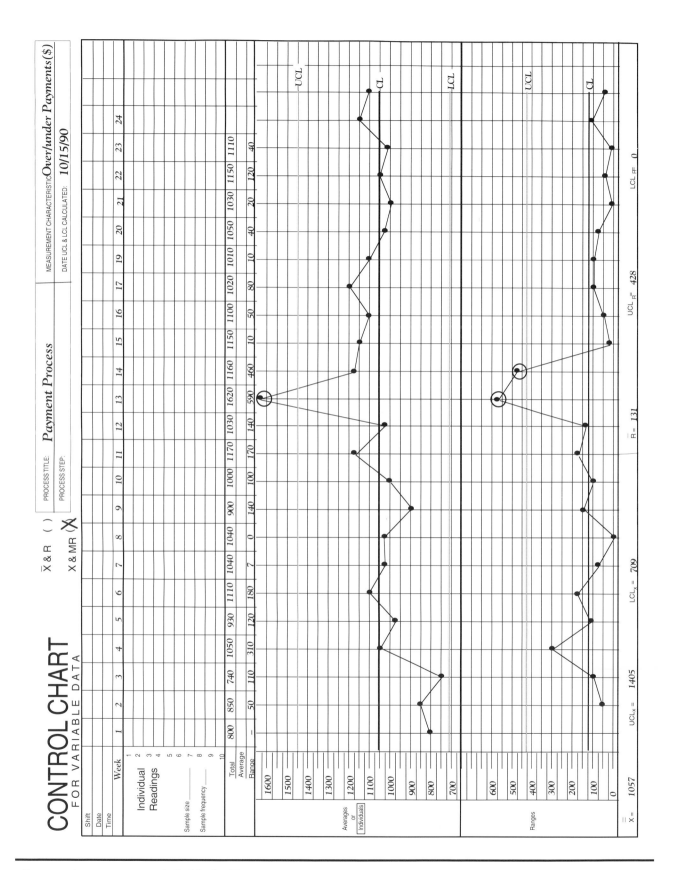

(For use with $\bar{X}$ and R charts and X and MR charts)

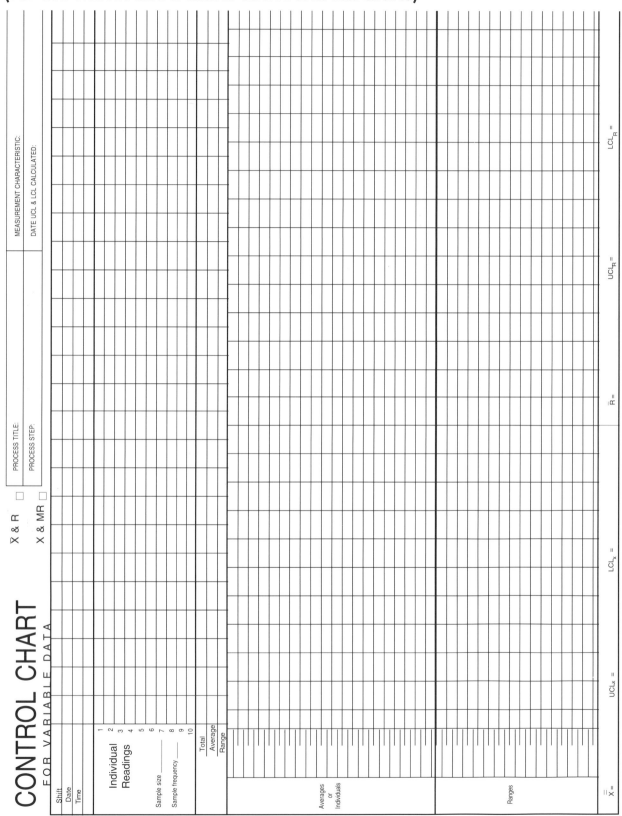

CONTROL CHART
FOR VARIABLE DATA

$\bar{X}$ & R ☐

X & MR ☐

PROCESS TITLE:

PROCESS STEP:

MEASUREMENT CHARACTERISTIC:

DATE UCL & LCL CALCULATED:

Shift
Date
Time

Individual
Readings

1
2
3
4
5
6
7
8
9
10

Sample size ____

Sample frequency ____

Total
Average
Range

Averages
or
Individuals

Ranges

$\bar{\bar{X}} =$ $UCL_X =$ $LCL_X =$ $\bar{R} =$ $UCL_R =$ $LCL_R =$

X and MR Control Chart Worksheet

1. You'll analyze the moving range (MR) chart first and the individual variables (X) chart second.

2. Compute the moving range (MR) for each subgroup.

3. Scale the MR portion of the chart (the lower portion).

4. Compute the average of the MR values (called $\overline{MR}$) by adding all of the MR values and dividing the total by the number of MR values.

$$\overline{MR} = (MR_1 + MR_2 + ... + MR_{(k-1)}/(k-1) = \underline{\hspace{2cm}}$$

5. Compute the moving range upper control limit (UCL_{MR}) by multiplying $\overline{MR}$ times 3.268.

$$UCL_{MR} = 3.268 \times \overline{MR} = \underline{\hspace{4cm}}$$

6. Draw the upper and lower control limits computed in steps 4 and 5 on the MR chart.

7. Scale the vertical axis of the X portion of the control chart (upper portion) and plot the X points.

8. In preparation for computing the upper and lower control limits in steps 9 and 10, compute $\overline{X}$ for all the X values.

$$\overline{X} = (X_1 + X_2 + ... + X_k)/k = \underline{\hspace{3cm}}$$

9. Compute the upper control limit for X values (UCL_X) using the following formula:

$$UCL_X = \overline{X} + (3 \times [\overline{MR}/1.128]) = \underline{\hspace{3cm}}$$

10. Compute the lower control limit for the X values (LCL_X) using the following formula:

$$LCL_X = \overline{X} - (3 \times ([\overline{MR}/1.128]) = \underline{\hspace{3cm}}$$

11. Draw the upper and lower control limits computed in steps 9 and 10 on the X chart.

Subgroup Number	Number of Invoices	Number of Missing Reports
1	50	6
2	52	7
3	50	4
4	55	3
5	50	6
6	50	12
7	55	7
8	50	1
9	50	1
10	54	2
11	55	4
12	50	13
13	51	3
14	50	3
15	50	2
16	50	3
17	49	2
18	50	4
19	52	7
20	55	5

p (Proportion Defective) Control Chart

A p chart should be used for plotting attribute data — for example, defects or errors, as a proportion of the "opportunity" to have a defect or error.

The statistics of probability are somewhat different for attribute data than for variable data. Consequently, you'll notice that the formulas for computing control limits are quite different from the $\overline{X}$ and R and the X and MR charts. Also, the use of range charts (R or MR) is not applicable to attribute data so there is only one plot on a p control chart.

To illustrate a p chart, refer again to the team that's studying the financial management process described on page 88. In this case, the team has collected data to determine how often receiving reports are missing from the company's files. Team members chose a p chart because they wanted to represent invoices that can't be matched with missing receiving reports as a proportion of all the invoices the company processes.

The team collected data for 20 consecutive working days. They identified the total number of invoices processed each day and the number of invoices for which no receiving report could be found in company files. The team's results are shown above.

The calculations necessary to develop the control lines of the p chart are given below. Step 10 contains the formula for estimating the standard deviation of attributes expressed as a proportion. Step 5 and 6 simply add three standard deviations to either side of the center line, p, to arrive at the control limits.

The completed chart on page 184 shows that, in the example, two points are out of control. As stated in step 7, these points should be investigated and the control lines recomputed if necessary.

How to Use

1. Compute the proportion defective (p) for each subgroup. Let's use subgroup 1 as an example. Subgroup 1 shows that there are 50 recordings and 6 are defective. In this case, the proportion defective is computed by dividing 6 by 50, 6/50, which is .12. To change .12 from a decimal, multiply it by 100. As we have just shown, 6/50 equals .12, and this is the same as 12 percent, that is, 6 is 12 percent of 50.

2. Scale the chart so that you can plot the largest and the smallest values of p (computed in step 1) and then plot the points.

3. Compute the average value of all the p values ($\bar{p}$) by adding all the separate subgroup p's together and dividing by the number of subgroups.

$$\bar{p} = (X_1 + X_2 + ... + X_k)/(n_1 + n_2 + ... + n_k) = .092$$

Where X = the number of defects; n = the number of values in the sample, or if all n are equal: $\bar{p} = (p_1 + p_2 + ... + p_k)/k =$ (where k = the number of subgroups).

4. Plot $\bar{p}$ computed in step 3 as a solid line on the chart on page 184.

5. In preparation for computing the upper and lower control limits for p, compute the average of n ($\bar{n}$), which is the total of all the measurements divided by the number of measurements.

$$\bar{n} = (n_1 + n_2 + ... + n_k)/k = 51.4$$

6. As a second step in preparation for computing the upper and lower control limits for p, compute the standard deviation (a statistical term that helps describe how data are spread) for p using the formula below. This may look confusing and difficult, but if you follow the steps in the order listed, you'll get the answer you need.

- Subtract $\bar{p}$ from 1 and then multiply this value by $\bar{p}$.

- Divide the number above by $\bar{n}$.

- Take the square root of the number immediately above. The answer you get is one standard deviation (s_p) for the data collected.

- The formula for the above looks like this:

$$s_p = \frac{\sqrt{\bar{p}(1-\bar{p})}}{\bar{n}}$$

$$= \sqrt{.092 \times (1-.092)/51.4}$$

$$= .0403$$

7. Compute the upper control limit for p (UCL_p) using the formula below:

$$UCL_p = \bar{p} + (3 \times s_p) = .092 + (3 \times .0403) = .213$$

8. Compute the lower control limit for p (LCL_p) using the formula below:

$$LCL_p = \bar{p} - (3 \times s_p) = .092 - (3 \times .0403) = -.029$$

Note: $LCL_p = 0$ if the above calculation results in a negative number.

9. Draw the upper and lower control limits computed in steps 7 and 8.

If any of the plotted points exceed either of the control lines, and if you know why this occurred (that is, you are able to identify the special cause of this abnormal variation), remove the identified point from the data set and recompute and plot the data using steps 1 through 9 above. If you don't know the special causes associated with the point(s) that is/are out of control, conduct further investigations. If you still can't find the special cause(s), leave the points as they are.

p Control Chart Worksheet

How to Use

1. Compute the proportion defective (p) for each subgroup.

2. Scale the chart so that you can plot the largest and the small-est values of p (computed in step 1) and then plot the points.

3. Compute the average value of all the p values ($\overline{p}$) by adding all the separate subgroup p's together and dividing by the number of subgroups.

$$\overline{p} = (X_1 + X_2 + ... + X_k)/(n_1 + n_2 + ... + n_k) =$$

    _____

4. Plot $\overline{p}$ computed in step 3 as a solid line on the chart on page 184.

5. In preparation for computing the upper and lower control limits for p, compute the average of n ($\overline{n}$), which is the total of all the measurements divided by the number of measure-ments.

$$\overline{n} = (n_1 + n_2 + ... + n_k)/k = \underline{\hspace{5cm}}$$

6. As a second step in preparation for computing the upper and lower control limits for p, use the formula below to compute the standard deviation.

*   Subtract $\overline{p}$ from 1 and then multiply this value by $\overline{p}$.

    _____

*   Divide the number above by $\overline{n}$. $\underline{\hspace{4cm}}$

*   Take the square root of the number immediately above. The answer you get is one standard deviation (s_p) for the data col-lected. $\underline{\hspace{5cm}}$

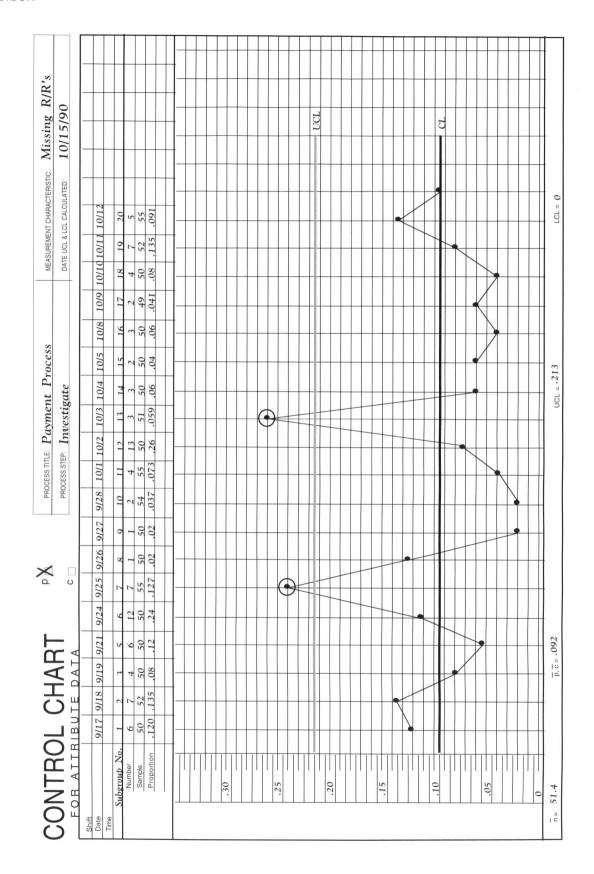

CONTROL CHART
FOR ATTRIBUTE DATA

p ☒   c ☐

PROCESS TITLE: *Payment Process*

PROCESS STEP: *Investigate*

MEASUREMENT CHARACTERISTIC: *Missing R/R's*

DATE UCL & LCL CALCULATED: *10/15/90*

Subgroup No.	1	2	3	4	5	6	7	8	9	10	11	12	13	14	15	16	17	18	19	20
Date	9/17	9/18	9/19	9/21	9/24	9/25	9/26	9/27	9/28	10/1	10/2	10/3	10/4	10/5	10/8	10/9	10/10	10/11	10/12	
Number	6	7	4	6	12	7	1	1	2	4	13	3	3	2	3	2	4	7	5	
Sample	50	52	50	50	50	55	50	50	54	55	50	51	50	50	50	49	50	52	55	
Proportion	.120	.135	.08	.12	.24	.127	.02	.02	.037	.073	.26	.059	.06	.04	.06	.041	.08	.135	.091	

$\bar{n} = 51.4$

$\bar{p}, \bar{c} = .092$

UCL = .213

LCL = 0

.30
.25
.20
.15
.10
.05
0

- The formula for the above looks like this:

$$s_p = \sqrt{p\,(1-p)/n} =$$

$$s_p = \underline{\hspace{10cm}}$$

7. Compute the upper control limit for p (UCL_p) using the formula below:

$$UCL_p = p + (3 \times s_p) = \underline{\hspace{6cm}}$$

8. Compute the lower control limit for p (LCL_p) using the formula below:

$$LCL_p = p - (3 \times s_p) = \underline{\hspace{6cm}}$$

Note: $LCL_p = 0$ if above calculation is negative.

9. Draw the upper and lower control limits computed in steps 7 and 8.

c-Control Chart Table

Subgroup Number	Number of Defectives
1	8
2	9
3	5
4	8
5	5
6	9
7	9
8	11
9	8
10	7
11	6
12	4
13	7
14	6
15	14
16	6
17	4
18	11
19	7
20	8
21	18
22	6
23	9
24	10
25	5

c (Individual Counted Defects) Control Chart

The c chart should be used when:

- counting the total number of defects present in production or service

- discrete attributes (defects) occur within some finite region of space, period of time, or product

- The opportunity for defects to occur in a product or service is great, but the number of defects that actually occur is small

As you review the instructions for computing the c chart's control limits, you'll see that this chart is the easiest of the four types of control charts to construct. The estimate of the standard deviation for the type of data contained in c charts is simply $\sqrt{\bar{c}}$ the control limits are set at three standard deviations on either side of $\bar{c}$.

In this case, the financial management team decided to monitor the number of hours lost each month due to computer downtime. Since the total number of hours in a month outweighed the amount of time computers were down during that period, the team decided that the best way to monitor the situation was to count the numbers of actual computer downtime hours that occurred each month.

The team collected results for the past 25 months, as shown in the table on this page.

As you can see from the completed c chart shown on page 189, the team found that one point was out of control.

How to Use

1. Scale the vertical axis of the control chart so that the smallest and the largest number of defects can be plotted on the chart.

2. Plot the number of defects (c) for each measurement period.

3. Compute the average number of defects for the process ($\bar{c}$)

by adding the defects for each measurement period together and dividing by the number of measurement periods. Plot this line on the chart and label it the center line (CL).

$$\bar{c} = (c_1 + c_2 + ... + c_k)/k = 8.0$$

Where k is the number of subgroups.

4. Compute the upper control limit for c using the formula below:

$$UCL_c = \bar{c} + 3\sqrt{\bar{c}}$$

$$= 8.0 + (3 \times \sqrt{8.0})$$

$$= 16.5$$

5. Compute the lower control limit for c using the formula below:

$$LCL_c = \bar{c} - 3\sqrt{\bar{c}}$$

$$= 8.0 - 3(\sqrt{8.0})$$

$$= -.5$$

$$= 0$$

6. Draw the upper and lower control limits computed in steps 4 and 5.

If any of the plotted points exceed either of the control lines, and if you know why this occurred (that is, you are able to identify the special cause of this abnormal variation), remove the identified point from the data set and recompute and plot the data using steps 1 through 6. If you don't know the special causes associated with the point(s) that is/are out of control, conduct further investigations. If you still can't find the special cause(s), leave the points as they are.

The c (Individual Counted Defects) Control Chart Worksheet

1. Scale the vertical axis of the control chart so that the smallest and the largest number of defects can be plotted on the chart.

2. Plot the number of defects (c) for each measurement period.

3. Compute the average number of defects for the process ($\bar{c}$) by adding the defects for each measurement period together and dividing by the number of measurement periods. Plot this line on the chart and label it the center line (CL).

$$\bar{c} = (c_1 + c_2 + ... + c_k)/k = \underline{\hspace{3in}}$$

4. Compute the upper control limit for c using the formula below:

$$UCL_c = \bar{c} + 3\sqrt{\bar{c}} = \underline{\hspace{3in}}$$

5. Compute the lower control limit for c using the formula below:

$$LCL_c = \bar{c} - 3\sqrt{\bar{c}} = \underline{\hspace{3in}}$$

6. Draw the upper and lower control limits computed in steps 4 and 5.

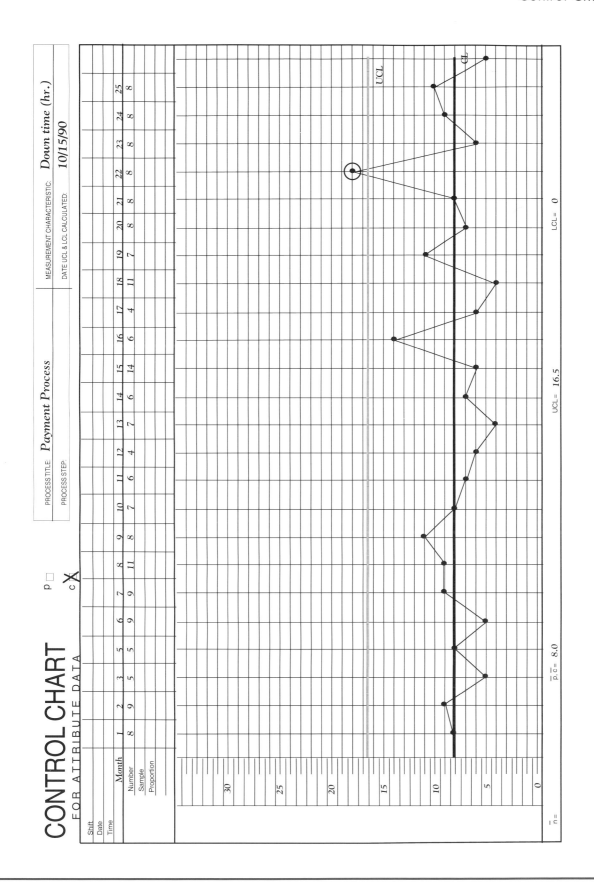

CONTROL CHART
FOR ATTRIBUTE DATA

p □

c X

PROCESS TITLE: *Payment Process*

PROCESS STEP:

MEASUREMENT CHARACTERISTIC: *Down time (hr.)*

DATE UCL & LCL CALCULATED: *10/15/90*

Month	1	2	3	4	5	6	7	8	9	10	11	12	13	14	15	16	17	18	19	20	21	22	23	24	25
Number	8	9	5	5	5	9	9	11	8	7	6	4	7	6	14	6	4	11	7	8	8	8	8	8	8
Sample																									
Proportion																									

Shift

Date

Time

UCL

CL

$\bar{n} =$

$\bar{p}, \bar{c} = 8.0$

UCL = 16.5

LCL = 0

(For use with c and p charts)

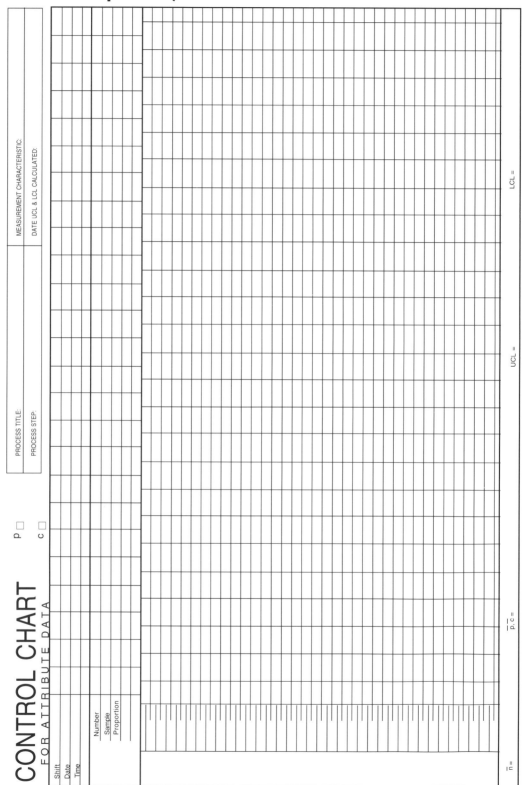

CONTROL CHART
FOR ATTRIBUTE DATA

Shift
Date
Time

Number
Sample
Proportion

p ☐
c ☐

PROCESS TITLE:
PROCESS STEP:

MEASUREMENT CHARACTERISTIC:
DATE UCL & LCL CALCULATED:

$\bar{p}, \bar{c} =$
$\bar{n} =$

UCL =
LCL =

Deployment Chart

Like a top-down flowchart (see page 228), a deployment chart displays the steps involved in a process in sequential order, but deployment charts also illustrate where each step is performed and who is involved. For example, instead of illustrating that logging-in a document is simply the first step in a process, the deployment chart shown here also indicates that a person with a specific job description — namely, a clerk — performs this step.

Process Steps	Clerk	Supervisor	Input Operator	Scheduler
Log in document	X			
Sort	X			
Review for corrections		X		
Data entry			X	
Assignment to purchasing team				X
Review		X		
Distribution	X			

Use a deployment chart instead of a top-down flowchart when you want to illustrate:

- who does what at a certain point in the process

- where each step is performed

- the distance that work must travel between steps

- points where work flows out of and back into the process you're seeking to improve

How to Use

1. Establish the boundaries of your process.

2. List each of the steps in sequential order.

3. The horizontal axis is often used to show where each step is performed. If a small process is involved, you could choose, as in the illustration, to indicate who performs each step. If you're seeking to examine a larger process, you may wish to show which work teams or functions are involved at different points in the process. Determine what you wish to know and

then decide how to identify the locations, people, or work groups involved.

4. Draw columns down the page and label each column with either the positions that people involved in the process hold or the locations of places where specific steps in the process are performed.

5. For each step, place a mark (such as an X or a check) in the correct column to indicate where or by whom the step is performed.

6. Connect the marks to illustrate the process flow.

Helpful Hints

*   Keep it simple. Use as few words as possible to label columns and describe work steps.

*   If work flows outside your process for some reason and then comes back again, you can show it in several ways:

-   Create a separate column and label it "outside."

-   Create one or more columns and label each specifically using such headings as "Department Head," "Fulfillment," "Engineering," etc.

-   Note the external work that gets done in the space outside the boundaries of your chart. You should indicate what happens and who is involved. Use lines to indicate where the work leaves and returns to your process.

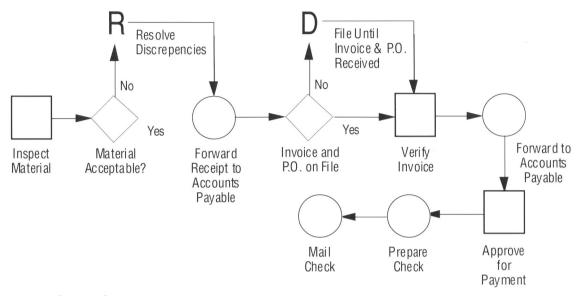

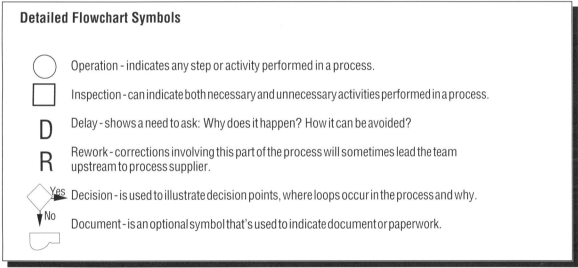

Detailed Flowchart

Detailed flowcharts show the process as it really happens. All steps are documented in sequential order, and a variety of symbols can be used to illustrate process flow, decision points, delays, and re-work. (See illustration above)

Detailed flowcharts generally take a lot of time to prepare, but they can be very useful. Because they show how a process actually works, detailed flowcharts can help teams identify problems, causes of problems, and streamlining opportunities.

How to Use

1. Agree on how detailed the flowchart should be. If your process is small, you may be able to capture most or all of it on paper. If your process is large, you may want to exclude, for purposes of convenience, some detail that doesn't add value to your team's understanding of the process.

2. Agree on the set of symbols you will use to represent steps, decisions, delays, etc.

3. Identify each process-related activity as it actually occurs, in the order it occurs. To do this you should repeatedly ask "What happens next?"

4. Select the right symbol for each action and use it, along with a brief description, to record the step.

5. Use arrows to indicate how the process flows from one activity to another.

6. When you've completed the chart, review and edit it as necessary, reproduce it, and distribute it to team members.

Helpful Hints

- Don't construct a new flowchart of your process if one already exists. Even if it's outdated, revising the chart is easier than starting from scratch.

- Consider using sticky notes or a dry-eraser board when first constructing the flowchart. Changes are inevitable. Using sticky notes enables you to move process steps around with ease.

- Avoid too much detail. Don't spent a lot of time making the flowchart look impressive. Teams can get bogged down in the process of perfecting it, so don't waste time this way.

Force Field Analysis

This highly versatile tool, first developed by social psychologist Kurt Lewin, can help your team reality-test ideas. Use force field analysis to subject ideas to hard scrutiny before recommending them to management.

You can also use force field analysis to maximize the strengths of your ideas or minimize their weaknesses. For example, let's suppose you want to pay invoices within 14 days after receiving them so that you can reduce administrative and late payment costs and improve customer satisfaction.

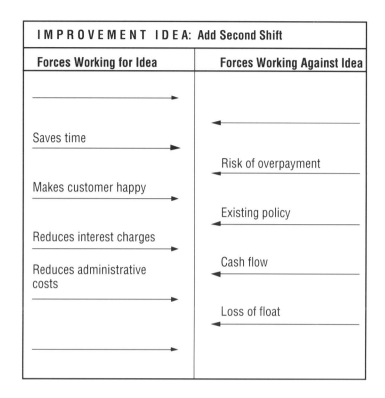

IMPROVEMENT IDEA: Add Second Shift	
Forces Working for Idea	**Forces Working Against Idea**
Saves time	Risk of overpayment
Makes customer happy	Existing policy
Reduces interest charges	Cash flow
Reduces administrative costs	Loss of float

There's a hitch, however. A small percentage of the invoices you pay involve high-cost items. Paying for them earlier than you do now may create a conflict with your organizations's cash flow policies. Force field analysis can help you modify your idea to include an exception pertaining to high-dollar invoices. That way, everyone involved stands a better chance of accepting and benefiting from your idea.

How to Use

1. Select an improvement idea to evaluate and explain how it would work under ideal conditions.

2. List all of the driving forces affecting that solution. (Driving forces are preconditions that work for the acceptance and success of the improvement.)

3. List all of the restraining forces affecting the solution. (Restraining force are preconditions that work against the acceptance or success of the improvement.)

4. Review your list of restraining forces. Can you eliminate any? Can you minimize them? How? (Consider strategies for eliminating or reducing the significance of each of the restraining forces you've identified.)

5. Review your list of driving forces. Can any be reinforced or made more significant? How? Can you think of or establish any additional driving forces? What will it take to do so? Consider strategies for reinforcing or increasing the number of driving forces.

Helpful Hints

Here are some issues to consider as you explore the strengths and weaknesses of each of your ideas:

- Management commitment — can you develop support for your idea?

  - key managers

  - commitment of key managers

- Strategic factors — are they reflected in your approach?

  - organizational values

  - existing organizational strategy

- Operating and management systems - does your idea complement these or conflict with them?

  - decision-making systems

  - accounting systems

  - communication systems

- reward systems

- The organization's culture — how can your idea best achieve acceptance from others?

    - morale

    - trust

    - communication, cooperation

    - openness, risk-taking

- Environment — what kinds of constraints may have an impact on whether or not your idea is accepted?

    - political

    - budget, financial

    - legal, regulatory

Gantt Chart

Named after its early 20th-century developer Henry L. Gantt, the Gantt chart is used to show what tasks you need to do, who will be responsible for doing them, and in what time frame they must be accomplished.

Teams use this tool to present their recommendations to management. It is designed to provide management with an understanding of what is required to implement such recommendations.

Activities	Jan '93					Feb '93				Mar '93		
	3	10	17	24	31	7	14	21	28	7	14	21
1 Orient Groups												
2 Train Operators												
3 Order Equipment												
4 Install Equipment												
5 Stockpile Spares												
6 Implement System												
7 Install Measures												
8 Monitor Results												

How to Use

1. Identify all the tasks that need to be completed in order to implement your team's recommendations for improvement.

2. Decide in what sequence the tasks should be completed.

3. Estimate the amount of time each task will take to complete and determine when each task should begin and end.

4. Develop a chart. List the tasks you've selected and the people responsible for them on the vertical axis. List the time frames you've chosen on the horizontal axis in whatever increment is appropriate — days, weeks, months, etc.

5. Plot the appropriate time frames for each task on the chart. When completed, the Gantt chart should clearly outline what is required, when it is required, and who is responsible for implementing it.

Helpful Hints

*   Make sure that the tasks you've outlined can be achieved during the time frame you've suggested

*   It's always a good idea to prepare a contingency plan just in case something develops that interferes with your implementation plan.

Table of Measures

9.9	9.5	9.8	9.9	10.4
9.6	9.4	9.3	9.4	10.6
10.2	10.2	10.4	10.0	10.3
10.1	9.7	9.7	9.7	10.1
9.7	9.5	9.8	9.8	10.1
9.7	9.7	9.3	9.5	9.9
9.8	9.8	9.9	9.8	9.9
9.2	9.3	9.3	9.3	9.7
9.6	9.5	9.4	9.5	9.6
10.2	9.9	9.2	9.0	10.0
9.7	9.6	9.9	9.4	9.7
10.1	10.2	9.7	9.5	10.3
9.9	9.8	9.8	9.4	9.5
9.9	10.0	9.9	10.1	10.7
9.8	10.0	10.0	9.6	10.2
10.3	9.7	10.0	10.1	10.1
9.5	9.8	9.8	9.8	9.9
9.6	10.2	9.7	9.9	9.7
9.8	9.9	9.6	9.8	10.0
9.8	9.7	9.6	9.5	9.8
10.3	9.3	9.3	9.6	10.1
10.2	9.4	9.8	10.0	10.0
10.0	9.5	9.6	9.6	10.3
10.3	9.7	9.7	10.0	10.7
10.1	9.8	10.0	10.1	10.7

Histogram

A histogram is a special kind of bar chart that's used to understand and illustrate variation. Because it presents a picture of variation in a data set, several pieces of information become immediately apparent in a way that they couldn't in a table or spreadsheet.

For example, the histogram illustrates measures of central tendency — a clustering of the values found in a statistical distribution. These include the mean (the average of all of the values contained in a data set), the median (a midpoint in the data; one-half of the values contained in a set of data are above this value and one-half are below it), and the mode (the value that occurs most frequently in a set of data). The histogram also clearly shows the range of variation found around the most frequently occurring or expected values. Finally, a histogram helps a team determine if the distribution of the data is normal or abnormal.

The histogram is easy to construct and provides a simple, easy-to-read summary of a distribution's central tendency and total variation. Use this tool when you need to understand the variation in your process in order to improve it.

Histogram

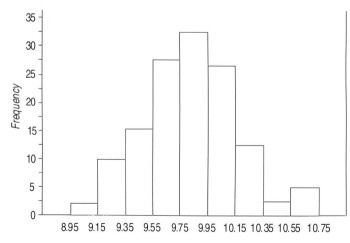

Measured Characteristics

How to Use

Once you've collected some data, construct a histogram by following the ten steps outlined below:

1. Count the number of individual measures you've collected. The number of individual measures or data points is referred to as n. In the table of measures shown above, we collected 125 measures, so n = 125.

Frequency Table

2. Determine the range (R) by subtracting the smallest value from the largest value. Here, the smallest value is 9 and the largest is 10.7, so R = 10.7 – 9, or 1.7.

Class Number	Class Boundaries	Frequency of Observations from the Data Set	Frequency Total
1	8.95 - 9.15	I	1
2	9.15 - 9.35	IIII IIII	9
3	9.35 - 9.55	IIII IIII IIII I	16
4	9.55 - 9.75	IIII IIII IIII IIII IIII II	27
5	9.75 - 9.85	IIII IIII IIII IIII IIII IIII I	31
6	9.95 - 10.15	IIII IIII IIII IIII II	22
7	10.15 - 10.35	IIII IIII III	13
8	10.35 - 10.55	II	2
9	10.55 - 10.75	IIII	4

3. Now determine the number of classes (k) into which you will divide the data. There's no precisely correct number, but the sampling table shown here does provide some guidelines.

Since n = 125, any number of classes between 7 and 12 can be used. Here, 9 is used.

4. Next, by applying the formula shown here, you need to determine how wide (w) the classes should be. In this example, the range (R) is 1.7 and 9 was selected as the number of classes (k), so the class width (w) = 1.7/9, or 0.189. You'll need to round this number up so that it has the same number of decimal points as the data. Since the data are expressed in tenths, round w up to 0.2.

Sampling Table

n	k
Under 50	5 - 7
50 - 100	6 - 10
100 - 250	7 - 12
Over 250	10 - 20

5. Now that you know how wide (w) each class (k) will be, you will need to determine the actual values that will define each class width. To avoid confusion, you should establish boundaries so that every individual measure falls clearly within one class or the other, not on a boundary line. One way to do that is to establish the class boundaries at one level "below" your data. If, for example, your data are expressed in whole numbers, establish class boundaries using tenths. Since the data in this example are expressed in tenths, we'll establish class boundaries using hundredths.

6. Divide .1 (since the data are expressed in tenths) by 2 to get .05. Subtracting this number from the lowest individual measure (9.0) gives us 8.95. This results in a low boundary, expressed in hundredths, for your first class.

7. To determine the high boundary for your first class, add the width (.2) to get 8.95 + .2 = 9.15.

8. Determine the boundaries for each remaining class by adding the width to the high boundary of the preceding class. For example, .2 + 9.15 = 9.35.

9. Construct a frequency table. (The one shown on page 201 corresponds to our example.) Count the number of individual measures you've made that fall into each class and record them as shown.

10. The last step is simply to draw the bar graph based on your frequency table.

Helpful Hints

- You need a minimum of 50 data points to construct a meaningful histogram.

- Don't worry too much about precision when you're constructing a histogram — it's a tool for estimating variation, not pinpointing it.

Idealized Redesign

Idealized redesign is a technique for helping individuals or groups to escape self-imposed constraints. When you start with the "as is" and try to improve a process, it is often difficult to see beyond the assumptions you've built up during your everyday involvement with that process. These assumptions limit people's ability to visualize anything more than minor revisions of the process, even though real improvement often involves doing things in radically different ways.

Idealized redesign seeks to put aside the process as it currently exists. The object of this idea-generating game is to fix in your mind the key objectives of the process (what does it exist to do?) and then think of what would be involved in making your ideal version of that process work. In essence, you design a desirable future and then look for ways to achieve it.

In order to escape the normal constraints that limit creativity, your redesign efforts should be subjected to only two constraints. First, your ideas or process characteristics should be technically feasible, although this does not preclude innovation. Second, the process you design should be capable of being or becoming operational.

Here's an example of the technique that Russell Ackoff, author of *The Art of Problem Solving*, used in 1978. It involves an idealized redesign of the telephone. After citing all the deficiencies in the then-current telephone system, he thought about the purpose of the telephone and listed the following as ideal characteristics of a telephone system.

- I could use the phone without using my hands.

- I would be able to carry the phone with me.

- I would be informed of who was calling me before I answered the phone.

- I would be able to hold conference calls.

- I would be able to leave messages for specific callers when they are not available to receive their calls.

In 1978, few, if any, of these capabilities existed. Yet they were all technologically feasible and, in fact, they are all available today. You, too, can use this technique to broaden your team's perspective and promote creative thinking.

How to Use

1. List the major problems of or complaints about your process that have been voiced by customers, managers, or process operators.

2. Put your list of problems aside for a moment and consider the purpose for your process. Why does it exist? Review your customers' expectations if you need clarification. Review your process outputs as well.

3. Imagine that your process could be whatever you wanted it to be. (Don't forget your constraints.) List some characteristics of this ideal process.

4. Compare your two lists and look for ideas on your second list that don't emerge logically from a focus on problems.

5. Look for potential solutions in some of the more promising characteristics of your ideal process. Use brainstorming, solution-mapping, or other idea-generation techniques. How can you make it happen? Can the idea be modified to meet present circumstances? What new alternatives does this perspective open up?

Helpful Hints

• Plan an idealized redesign to enhance the qualities of your work. During a team meeting, agree on the purposes for your process. Schedule a redesign session for the next meeting. During the period between meetings, all team members should think about the ideal characteristics of the process, write them down, and bring their lists to the next meeting.

- Discuss the design constraints your process has before conducting a session.

- Write the purposes for your process on a board or flipchart, so that all team members can see them.

- Use a cause-and-effect diagram (see page 160), tree diagram (see page 230), or solution map (see page 226) to generate ideas on how to implement promising characteristics. What must happen to cause your ideal characteristics to become a reality?

Multi-voting

Multi-voting is a kind of "process of elimination" group voting technique. It is used to focus a team's energy so that they can separate essential items from a larger list of potentially useful items. Use multi-voting after brainstorming problems, causes, or improvement ideas.

How to Use

1. Determine precisely what the team is voting on. Find out, for example, whether it is expressing a preference for the most cost-effective ideas, the most practical, or for those that will most improve performance.

2. Give each team member a number of votes equal to approximately half the number of items on the list (for example, 10 votes for a 20-item list).

3. Make sure that each person knows that he or she may assign only one vote to a given item (in other words, team members vote for their personal top ten).

4. After one round of voting, drop items with few or no votes from the list.

5. If it is not clear what the top four to six items are at this point, do a second round of voting, assigning fewer votes per person (for example, 5 votes per person if the list now has 10 items).

Helpful Hints

• For most problems, a list of more than four to six items for further discussion and prioritization is unwieldy.

• After brainstorming, clean up your list of items — edit, combine, and eliminate duplication — before using multi-voting.

• Review the ideas you're evaluating to make sure everyone knows what they mean.

Nominal Group Technique

This technique, often called NGT, represents a more structured approach to generating ideas than either brainstorming or multi-voting. It is called a "nominal" group technique because during the session the "group" doesn't really engage in much interaction. NGT is an especially effective tool to use when all or some of the team's members are new to each other.

How to Use

1. Define the task in the form of a question.

2. Write the question on paper for everyone to see. Anyone who does not understand the question should be encouraged to ask for clarification.

3. Generate ideas by having team members write down their answers in silence.

4. List ideas by going around the room and having each participant read one idea from his or her list. Write down every answer on a flipchart and continue this "round robin" until everyone's list is complete or until time has run out.

5. Clarify and discuss the ideas the team has offered.

6. Condense the list as much as possible; if the originators of the ideas give their approval, combine similar ideas.

7. If there are more than 50 ideas, use the method of your choice to reduce the list to 50 or fewer ideas, if possible.

8. Give each participant four to eight cards. The number of cards is a rough fraction of the number of items still on the list. For example, give each participant four cards when up to 20 ideas have been generated, six cards when 20 to 35 ideas are involved, and eight cards when 35 to 50 ideas are involved.

9. Each team member, working alone, selects the best ideas from the list and writes one idea per card (four, six, or eight, depending on how many cards they have).

10. Team members assign a point value to each item, based on their preferences. Each person assigns the highest point value to the most important item. In an 80-card system, the most preferred item is numbered eight, the second most preferred item is numbered seven, and so on until the least preferred item is numbered one.

11. After each team member has assigned point values to the items he or she has selected, collect the cards and tally the points that each idea has received. Ideas with the highest point totals are the ones that the team collectively thinks are best.

Helpful Hints

- If your initial list of ideas is too large, try first to shorten the list by simply having the team determine which ideas can be quickly deleted.

- If necessary, use one or two rounds of multi-voting to reduce your list of ideas to 50 or fewer.

Opportunity Grid

An opportunity grid is a simple two-by-two matrix that can help your team clarify and illustrate customers' priorities. The grid identifies the expectations that customers have of your product or service and evaluates each of them in light of importance to customers and customers' satisfaction with your current performance in these areas.

It's best to use this tool when you're processing customer feedback. Use it to isolate customer expectations that are rated high in importance and low in satisfaction from others appearing in the grid. Once you've determined which expectations are the furthest from being met, you can begin to focus your efforts on those areas.

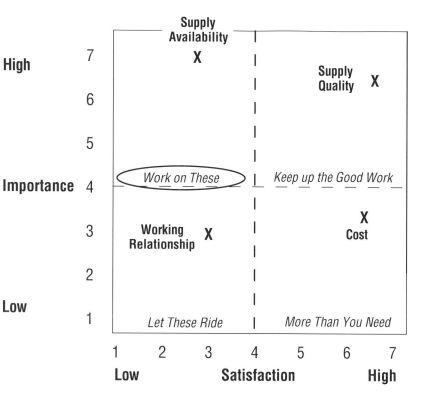

How to Use

1. Draw a square and divide it into four quadrants.

2. Identify each axis. The vertical axis indicates how important individual aspects of your process are, while the horizontal axis indicates how well your process is performing in each of these areas.

3. Scale each axis from 1 to 7.

4. Using your interview results, discuss each expectation and determine — by consensus — its appropriate location on the grid. In the example shown above, the availability of supplies shows itself to be very important to customers (5.75 on a

scale of 1 to 7). By contrast, however, customers rate the company's performance in this area as relatively unsatisfactory (2.5 on a scale of 1 to 7). In this case, the grid shows that there's clearly something to be gained by focusing on this problem.

Helpful Hints

- If your team has trouble reaching consensus, conduct individual votes for each of the customer expectations you've identified. Determine the average score of each expectation and plot it on the grid.

- Even when your team can clarify customer priorities without this tool, the opportunity grid can sometimes illustrate gaps between your priorities and your customers' priorities. For example, if your organization spends considerable resources to provide a service that customers don't value, then perhaps your priorities should change.

- Use an opportunity grid to help your team determine how to allocate resources more effectively. The grid might show you, for example, that some of the resources you use to keep the cost of a product down might be better spent on increasing the availability of suppliers.

- Consider including a completed opportunity grid in your final report to management.

Pairwise Ranking Matrix

Pairwise ranking techniques can be used by individuals or teams to prioritize a list of items. While there are many different variations of this technique, all of them have this in common — they force you to compare items — to rank each of them against each other. The combined results of these paired rankings help to clarify what the priorities of your team should be.

Use this tool whenever your team's preferences cannot be determined informally. If your list of items is larger than five, use multi-voting or a similar technique to reduce the list to five items before using this tool.

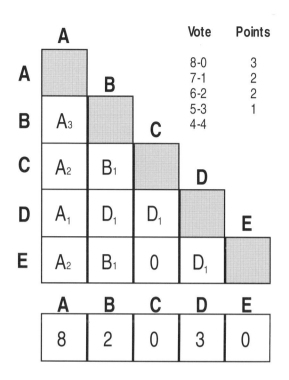

Vote	Points
8-0	3
7-1	2
6-2	2
5-3	1
4-4	

How to Use

1. Write the list of items you want to prioritize on a flipchart or board so that everyone can see them. Label them "A" through "E."

2. Draw a pairwise ranking matrix on a flipchart or board, or use an overhead projector and transparency. This matrix will be used to record the team's collective preferences, so it should be visible to everyone. Label the columns and rows A through E, as shown in the illustration above.

3. For each paired ranking, your team will indicate a preference for one item over the other. In order to further indicate the strength of each preference, you need to agree on a point system that gives more weight to strong preferences than to moderate or weak ones. If, for example, your team had eight members, you could use a point system like the one shown in the illustration.

4. Write the point system on a flipchart or board so everyone can see it.

5. Compare each item to every other item, one at a time. Notice that each unshaded square on the matrix represents the intersection between a column and row, which in turn are labeled to correspond to specific items on your list. Using a show of hands, the team should vote its preference for each possible comparison.

6. After each vote, the team leader should record the results by writing the letter (in the appropriate square) that indicates which item the team preferred and the number that shows the strength of the team's preference.

7. After completing all comparisons, count the total number of points assigned to each letter. The point totals will illustrate the team's collective preference.

Helpful Hints

*   One person should lead the voting and record the results of each comparison.

*   Be sure to clarify the items being compared in every case.

*   Start with the column marked "A." Ask "who prefers A over B?" "A over C?" and so on.

*   If there are tie votes, enter a zero in the corresponding squares.

Pareto Diagram

A Pareto diagram is a bar chart that's used to prioritize problems or the causes of problems. It is based on the proven principle that, while most problems have many contributing causes, most of the effect that these causes brought about can be traced to only a few of them. A Pareto diagram helps to isolate those vital few causes from other, less important ones.

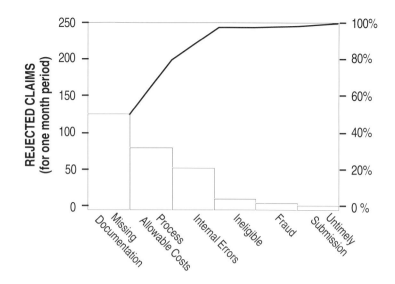

Pareto diagrams can be linked together at successive levels of detail to uncover a problem's root causes. In the example shown above, missing documentation is the most significant cause for rejected claims. A second Pareto diagram, shown on page 214, examines the problem at the next level of detail — it illustrates the causes of missing documentation.

How to Use

1. Select a problem or cause you want to analyze. In this case, we've selected rejected claims.

2. Decide on the time period you want to cover — a day, a week, a one-month period, etc.

3. Determine the categories that you'll use to further clarify your problem or issue; individual causes of the problem frequently serve as Pareto diagram categories. In the illustration, the reasons why claims are rejected are identified — missing documentation, exceeding allowable costs, and internal errors are the appropriate categories to use.

4. Decide how you will collect data. Do you already know the causes of your problem or will your organization's records indicate what they are? Will the records point clearly to one

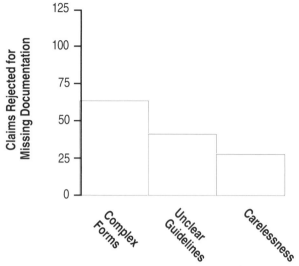

Claims Rejected for Missing Documentation (vertical axis: 0, 25, 50, 75, 100, 125)

Horizontal axis: Complex Forms, Unclear Guidelines, Carelessness

Legend
Data Drawn from Monthly Summary of Rejected Claims for Month of May, 1992

cause or another? Since a Pareto diagram uses data to prioritize causes for a problem, remember that you must clearly know how the data you gather will accomplish this objective before you collect it.

5. Design checksheets, if necessary, to help you collect data.

6. Collect the data.

7. Label and scale the left side of the vertical axis in accordance with the problems you're trying to solve — in other words, rejected claims. Scale the axis so that it corresponds with the data. For example, if the total number of rejected claims for a one-month period is 250, you could closely measure the scope of the problem by using a scale of 0–250 divided into increments of 50.

8. Draw a vertical axis on the far right side of the diagram. This axis, which represents percentages, will show you what percentage of the problem can be attributed to each of the causes you've listed on the horizontal axis. The bottom represents zero percent and the top represents 100 percent.

9. Draw a bar on the far left side of the diagram to show the impact of your most significant cause; in this case, we found that 120 claims were rejected for missing documentation.

10. Repeat step 8 for each additional cause. Arrange the cause bars in descending order, from the most significant cause to the least significant.

11. Draw a line, as shown in the first example, to illustrate the cumulative effect reached with the addition of each cause. In the example, the line has been drawn to illustrate that missing documentation and excess allowable costs account for 200 of the total 250 rejected claims.

12. Be sure that your diagram is labeled clearly.

Helpful Hints

- It's a good idea to list the source of the data, on which the diagram is based, in a legend, as shown on page 214.

- Instead of listing two or three lesser causes separately, you can combine them into a single bar and label it "other." This should always be the last bar on the right side of the diagram.

- It is not essential that your diagram show percentages and the cumulative effect of the many causes of a problem. When the data are straightforward and the effect is obvious, use a simpler diagram that lists only a problem and its causes.

Pie Chart

A pie chart is a commonly used type of graph that displays the relationship of each item you're considering to the broader topic under discussion.

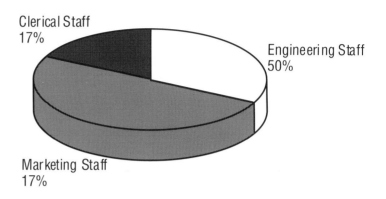

The 360 degrees of the circle or pie must represent the total number of factors involved, or 100 percent. Each pie chart that

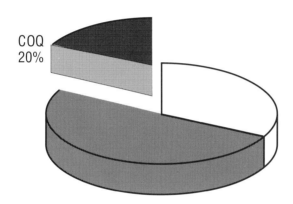

you construct must be divided into areas that reflect each component's percentage of the whole.

How to Use

1. Be sure that the focus of the pie chart, such as the example shown above, is displayed clearly.

2. You can use a pie chart to graphically illustrate only a portion of a total population. For example, the pie chart shown mid page depicts the

cost of quality (COQ) as a percentage of the total costs incurred by a company.

3. When you want to illustrate the division of a whole by percentages but you also want to specifically identify or qualify the entire population, you can draw a smaller circle inside the larger one. For example, the pie chart shown at the bottom of the page illustrates customer complaints received between June and December 1992 by category.

4. It is acceptable to collapse several categories representing small percentages of an entire population into a single category, using a general heading such as "other."

Helpful Hints

*   The use of color or shadings can make pie charts clearer and easier to read.

Review Board

Review boards are designed to help you ask for and receive feedback on your idea. Use this technique to reality-test ideas that the team feels strongly about.

Once you've applied force field analysis or other evaluation techniques, use a review board to take your evaluation one step further. Since a review board requires some time and effort, use it selectively (such as, for ideas that involve significant changes, increased costs).

How to Use

1. Describe your idea and present it as a proposal. Envision your reviewers (team members) as representatives of management who will decide whether to implement your idea and convince them that it's good. Provide sufficient details about the underlying assumptions of the idea, its projected cost and benefits, implementation-related issues, etc. Use charts and graphs if they will help.

If your idea turns out to be good and your team decides to recommend it, then all or most of the work you do here can be included in the final report you submit to management.

2. Select reviewers. There is no preferable way to select the individuals you'd like to evaluate your idea. You can elicit feedback from a few people who review your idea separately, or you can arrange for several people to act as a review board.

3. Determine the method of obtaining feedback that you'll use. There are many ways to do this but no one best way. You can make the feedback process informal and simple or more structured, depending on the nature and significance of your idea and on team preferences. Here are three options to consider:

   • Simple question method. Include in your proposal a list of questions for reviewers to answer. Request that reviewers meet with the team to discuss their evaluation, using the questions to structure the meeting.

Sample questions include:

- – Does the idea sound promising?

- – Do you agree with our assessment of cost and benefits?

- – Have we overlooked any significant risks?

- – It is the right time for this idea?

- – Where will resistance come from?

- – How can we neutralize it?

- – Does the idea have value?

- – Can you think of ways to improve the idea?

- Scoring method. Develop a scoring system to structure the feedback, using categories and providing a scoring range for each. Think through your decisions carefully and be sure to explain the procedures to review board members. For example, are all categories you've chosen equally important? If not, your scoring system should reflect your priorities. Here are a few sample categories you can use to organize the feedback you've received:

  - – presentation (organization, clarity, thoroughness, etc.)

  - – originality

  - – feasibility

  - – timing

  - – effectiveness

- General observations method. Ask the reviewers to indicate what they like most about your idea, what they like least, and what they would change.

4. Conduct evaluations. Be sure to state clearly what you want reviewers to do. Regardless of the method of feedback you select, you'll want to know if the idea has merit — and if so, how it can be improved.

Try to select people who you feel are:

*   imaginative (include people who can help you to improve your idea)

*   knowledgeable about the problem or situation

*   interested (include someone who is likely to be affected by the change)

*   capable of being objective about the problem or situation

Helpful Hints

*   Accept feedback from each individual nonjudgmentally. Record their observations. Ask questions to clarify their views or provide you with more information.

Run Chart

A run chart is a line graph that displays data related to a variable — such as time, cost, or productivity — in sequence over a period of time. The resulting picture enables you to quickly identify changes in performance over time and discover any trends or cycles in the data, which are indications of abnormal variation in your process. Therefore, a run chart can be used along with a histogram to understand process variation. See this page for a commuting time chart and table to show you how a run chart works.

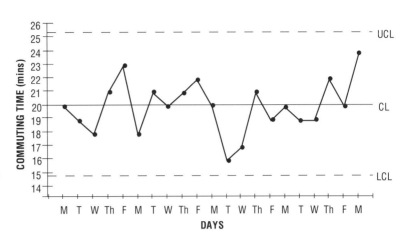

Commuting Time in Minutes (Jan)

Subgroup Number	Individual Values
1	20
2	19
3	18
4	21
5	23
6	18
7	21
8	20
9	21
10	22
11	20
12	16 = smallest
13	17
14	22
15	19
16	28
17	19
18	19
19	22
20	20
21	24 = largest

How to Use

1. Determine the range (R) for the data set by subtracting the smallest individual value of the data set from the largest value. For the "commuting time" data set on the right of the table, R = 24 – 16 = 8.

2. Scale the vertical axis of the run chart so that you can plot all your data. One way to do this is to:

-   Multiply the range of your data by 1.5. In this example, the range is 8, so 1.5 x 8 = 12.

-   Subtract the range value from your result and divide by 2. For example, $\frac{12 - 8}{2} = 2$

-   Add your result to the largest value in the data set to determine the top of the scale. For example, 2 + 24 = 26.

-   Subtract your result (2) from the smallest value in the data set to determine the bottom of the scale. For example, 16 – 2 = 14.

3. Label the vertical axis to indicate what you're measuring. In our example, the run chart measures the time, in minutes, that it takes to commute to work.

4. Label the horizontal axis with the appropriate time measure. You'll need to:

   - pick the right time increment to use — it could be minutes, hours, days, weeks, or months, depending on what you're measuring

   - determine the total length of time you want to measure — it could be a day, week, month, or even a year

   - label the horizontal axis clearly. In the example, daily commuting time for a four-week period is measured

5. Plot the points. In the example, one point is plotted to indicate the commuting time for each day indicated on the horizontal axis.

6. Connect the points with lines to clearly illustrate any patterns in the data.

Helpful Hints

- The data points plotted on a run chart can represent individual values (such as the number of minutes it takes to get to work), percentages, the number of errors that are committed, etc.

- Be sure to label your run chart clearly. If it illustrates commuting time for the month of January 1994, be sure that the graph is labeled as such. You'll prevent misunderstandings by being as clear and specific as you can.

- Remember, a run chart depicts time-sequenced data. Be sure to plot your points in order.

Scatter Diagram

A scatter diagram is a graph that uses paired data to depict the relationship, if any, between two issues (also referred to as variables). Each data point, indicated by a dot on the graph, represents a separate case (or situation) and shows the intersection of two variables that relate to that case. The dots plotted on the sample on this page represent individual projects; the graph examines a potential relationship between project delays and cost overruns. By collecting data and plotting many separate examples on a graph, you can determine if any two variables are related and, if so, how strong the relationship is.

Use a scatter diagram to confirm assumptions about a cause-and-effect relationship between two issues, especially when the implications are significant. If, for example, a costly recommendation rests on such an assumption of cause and effect, a scatter diagram can help you be sure that that relationship actually exists. It can also help to convince management, who must approve your recommendation of its validity.

Project Delays (weeks)		Cost Overruns (% budget)	
1. _____	13. _____	1. _____	13. _____
2. _____	14. _____	2. _____	14. _____
3. _____	15. _____	3. _____	15. _____
4. _____	16. _____	4. _____	16. _____
5. _____	17. _____	5. _____	17. _____
6. _____	18. _____	6. _____	18. _____
7. _____	19. _____	7. _____	19. _____
8. _____	20. _____	8. _____	20. _____
9. _____	21. _____	9. _____	21. _____
10. _____	22. _____	10. _____	22. _____
11. _____	23. _____	11. _____	23. _____
12. _____	24. _____	12. _____	24. _____
	25. _____		25. _____

How to Use

1. Determine how to collect the paired data required to investigate a possible relationship between two variables. In the example, individual project files have been chosen — they will identify cost overruns and delays for the project.

2. Collect data from at least 50 samples — project files, for example — and record the results on a table like the one shown above.

3. Draw the graph. Divide each axis into increments and label them accordingly. As you can see from the example, the vertical axis represents the potential effect (in this case, cost

overruns). The scale reflects the fact that overruns for sample projects ranged from 0 to 60 percent of the amount budgeted for them. The horizontal axis represents the potential cause (in this case, project delays). The scale used for the example shows that delays in projects ranged from 0 to 50 weeks.

4. Plot your data on the graph. Remember, each data point represents one case, which in turn contains a distinct value for each variable. If two cases have the same values for each variable — for example, a delay of 10 weeks and a cost overrun of 18 percent — they should occupy the same space on the graph. If this occurs, simply draw a circle around the point that is already plotted to indicate that a second data point also occupies that space. Use as many circles as required.

How to Test for a Relationship

When a relationship between two variables does exist, it's useful to know how strong it is. There are several methods for finding this out. The median method is best because it is the simplest and most practical. After you've constructed your scatter diagram, complete the following steps:

1. Determine the X median by drawing a horizontal line so that half the data points you've plotted are above the line and the other half are below it.

2. Determine the Y median by drawing a vertical line so that half the data points are to the left of the line and the other half are to the right of it.

3. You now have a graph divided into four quadrants. Label the quadrants "1," "2," "3," and "4," beginning with the top right quadrant and moving counterclockwise.

4. Count the total number of data points plotted on the graph. In the example on page 223, the total is 30.

5. Count the combined data points in quadrants 1 and 3. Don't count any data points falling on either median line. In the example, $P_{1,3} = 24$.

6. Count the combined data points in quadrants 2 and 4. Again, don't count any points falling on either median line. In the example, $P_{2,4} = 6$.

7. Determine the total number of points on the graph, minus any points falling on a median line. This value is referred to as n. In the example, n = 30.

8. Select the smallest of the two values $P_{1,3}$ and $P_{2,4}$ and label it PS. In the example, $P_{2,4}$ is the smallest, with a value of 6; therefore, PS = 6.

9. Determine the correct point limit (PL) from the sign table. The point limit is used to determine if a relationship exists between the variables. In the example, n = 30; therefore, PL = 9.

10. If PS is greater than PL, no relationship exists between the two variables. If PS is less than PL and $P_{1,3}$ is greater than $P_{2,4}$, a positive relationship exists between the two variables. That means they move in the same direction. The example used above fits both of these criteria: PS (6) is less than PL (9), and $P_{1,3}$ (24) is greater than $P_{2,4}$ (6). Therefore, we know that as project delays go up, cost overruns go up as well.

If PS is less than PL and $P_{2,4}$ is greater than $P_{1,3}$, then a negative relationship exists between the two variables. This means that, as the cause variable goes up, the effect variable goes down.

Sign Table

N	Point Limits (1&3) or (2&4)	N	Point Limits (1&3) or (2&4)
20	5	42	14
21	5	44	15
22	5	46	15
23	6	48	16
24	6	50	17
25	7	52	18
26	7	54	19
27	7	56	20
28	8	58	21
29	8	60	21
30	9	62	22
32	9	64	23
34	10	66	24
36	11	68	25
38	12	70	26
40	13		

Helpful Hints

- Plan ahead before you rush off to collect data. You may find it useful to review the five basic measurement plan-related questions outlined in Chapter IV on page 55. All of them won't apply to your situation, but a systematic review can help you think through your data collection requirements thoroughly.

Solution Map

Here's a technique you can use to structure a brainstorming session so that everyone gets involved. It also promotes free association and helps you to build on existing ideas — both of which are essential for a good brainstorming session.

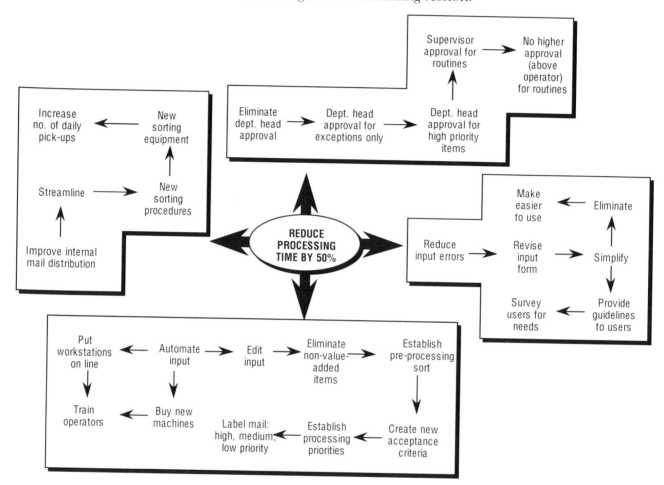

How to Use

1. Write your challenge on a flipchart, blackboard, or dry-eraser board. Rephrase the problem you are trying to solve in the form of a goal. Use a few words to describe that goal.

2. Allow team members to work independently for a few minutes. Have them jot down ideas that may help you to achieve your goal.

3. Start by getting one team member to offer an idea from his or her list. Write it on the flipchart or board. Use as few words as possible to describe each idea.

4. Move systematically around the room. Each team member should try to build on the previous idea. Use word association. Write each idea on the board as it is thrown out. Don't evaluate them! Allow each person 30 seconds to describe his or her idea.

5. If any team member can't come up with an idea within 30 seconds, he or she should offer one of the ideas from the written list. Continue to build on this new idea.

6. Continue the brainstorming session until all written ideas are covered.

7. After the session is completed, look for the main concepts that appear in your map. Draw arrows to connect related ideas. You can use geometric symbols (for example, squares, circles, diamonds, etc.) to identify similar ideas.

8. You can clean up your map and save it for later use or transfer your ideas to an outline format. Select the best ideas and evaluate their potential to solve the problem.

Helpful Hints

- One person should lead the session and serve as the team's scribe.

- Develop clusters of related ideas around the core challenge you've identified. When a team member can't build on an existing cluster but instead offers a new idea from his or her written list, start a new cluster.

- After getting started, allow participants to build on any idea already on the map instead of just the last one offered.

- If you don't have a large board, use sticky notes and a wall.

Top-Down Flowchart

A top-down flowchart uses words and shapes to create a simple picture of a process. The picture is presented using two levels of detail. The first level captures the major steps in the process, while the second level lists the "substeps" that fall under each major step.

A top-down flowchart summarizes how a process is supposed to work. It doesn't try to show all the delays, errors, rework, and decisions that most processes include, so it's easy to construct and doesn't take a lot of time. You don't need symbols or flowcharting tools to make this work.

Use a top-down flowchart to help your team clarify or confirm the sequential steps that occur in your process. A top-down flowchart is the right tool to use when you don't have a lot of time to spend on a flowchart, or when you want a clear, one-page summary of your process or aim to describe — not analyze — that process. The example below outlines the steps that are needed to complete a proposal-writing process.

How to Use

1. Agree on the start point and end point for the process.

2. Use four to eight major steps to describe the process from be-

Top-Down Flowchart

Plan For Proposal	Organize Proposal	Draft Proposal	Produce and Deliver
• Review RFP • Develop Strategy • Develop Milestone • Chart Assemble Team	• Identify Milestones • Outline Proposal • Questions • Make Assignments Identify Resources	• Gather Data • Draft Proposal • Sections • Assemble and Edit • Incorporate Graphics • Red Team	• Design Layout • Typeset • Paste-Up • Proof • Reproduction and • Building Delivery

ginning to end. List these steps horizontally across a dry-eraser board or a series of flipchart pages.

3. Break each major step into three to eight substeps. List the substeps under the corresponding major step.

4. Review your flowchart and make corrections as necessary. Rearrange steps, combine substeps, or revise the descriptions of major steps or substeps — for example, so that they most accurately describe the process.

5. Agree on a presentation format for the flowchart.

Helpful Hints

- Use as few words as possible to describe steps. If you do so, your flowchart will be easier to read.

- List only essential steps of the process. Don't try to record every little activity that takes place. Summarize the process using two levels of detail. Use the example on page 228 as a guide.

- There is no single correct number of major steps or substeps. Guidelines are offered here but they're not hard-and-fast rules.

- If a major step cannot be divided into at least three substeps, it probably can't be viewed as a major step.

- If a major step can be divided into more than eight substeps, it might turn to be two major steps, not one.

Tree Diagram

The tree diagram — also known by its more formal name, the systematic diagram — represents relationships graphically. It was developed to support a search for the most effective means of accomplishing a given objective.

It came by way of its informal name, the tree diagram, because it presents information in a way that resembles branches in a tree. The tree diagram is used to support a variety of analytical techniques, such as functional analysis, decision analysis, and cause-and-effect analysis.

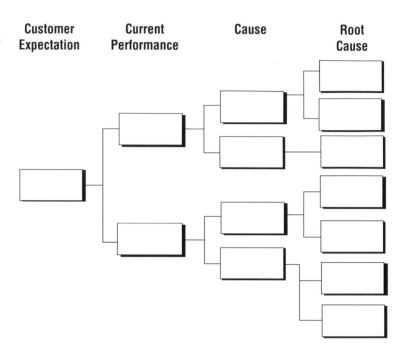

You can also use a tree diagram to help you confirm your assumptions about cause-and-effect relationships, particularly when you're not certain that your assumptions are especially significant.

How to Use

1. List what you believe are the root causes for the problem(s) you're studying.

2. Identify one or more levels of the intermediate causes that lead back to specific performance problem(s).

3. Define the specific performance problem(s).

4. Identify the related customer expectation(s).

5. Arrange the root causes, intermediate causes, performance problems, and customer expectations in a tree diagram, like the one shown above.

6. Discuss and verify the validity of your assumptions about the cause-and-effect relationship represented in the diagram.

Helpful Hints

- The performance problems you identify should relate to your key output characteristics.

- If possible, present your tree diagram to knowledgeable people who aren't on your team. They can bring a fresh insight to the issue and help you objectively evaluate your assumptions.

REFERENCES

Ackoff, Russell L. *The Art of Problem Solving.* New York: John Wiley & Sons, Inc., 1978.

Amsden, Robert T., Butler, Howard E., and Amsdem, Davida M. *SPC Simplified, Practical Steps to Quality.* White Plains, NY: Quality Resources, 1989.

Clark, Charles. *Brainstorming: How to Create Successful Ideas.* North Hollywood, CA: Melvin Powers Wilshire Book Company, 1958.

Ishikawa, Kaoru. *Guide to Quality Control.* Asian Productivity Organization, 1982.

Koontz, Harold, O'Donnell, Cyril, and Weihrich, Heinz. *Essentials of Management*, 3rd ed. New York: McGraw-Hill Book Company, 1982.

Lefevre, Henry L., ed. *Government Quality and Productivity — Success Stories.* Milwaukee, WI: ASQC Quality Press, 1992.

Michalko, Michael. *Thinker Toys.* Berkeley, CA: Ten Speed Press, 1991.

Mizuno, Shigeru, ed. *Management for Quality Improvement: The Seven New QC Tools.* Cambridge, MA: Productivity Press, 1988.

Stevens, Leigh. "Summoning Our Creative Powers." In *The Cutting Edge*, vol. 3, no. 2 (March/April 1988).

Thompson, Charles "Chic." *What a Great Idea — Key Steps Creative People Take.* New York: HarperPerennial, 1992.

Wheeler, Donald J., and Chambers, David S. *Understanding Statistical Process Control.* Knoxville, TN: Statistical Process Controls, Inc., 1986.

Yasuda, Yuzo. *40 Years, 20 Million Ideas: The Toyota Suggestion System.* Cambridge, MA: Productivity Press, 1991.

ABOUT THE AUTHORS

The authors of this second edition of *Process Improvement: A Guide for Teams* personally used the first edition in training and facilitating more than one hundred improvement teams in dozens of private and public organizations, which range from Fortune 500 companies to major defense and civilian agencies. Each is a Managing Associate in Coopers & Lybrand's (C&L) U.S. Center of Excellence for Total Quality Management in Washington, D.C.

Clifton M. Cooksey, CQA, directs product development for the Center of Excellence, and provides consulting and training services to C&L's TQM clients. He has been certified as a Quality Auditor by the American Society for Quality Control. Before joining C&L, he was a Navy officer and director of quality at the Pensacola, Florida, Naval Aviation Depot, as well as an aeronautical engineer and helicopter pilot. He is co-author of *Measuring Quality: Linking Customer Satisfaction to Process Improvement*, and articles on quality in *Training* and *Incentive*. Mr. Cooksey holds a B.S. degree in aerospace engineering from the U.S. Naval Academy and an M.S. in aeronautical engineering from the Naval Post Graduate School.

Richard L. Beans is a member of the Research and Development team at the Center of Excellence and provides consulting and training services to C&L's TQM clients. He has helped to design and develop many of the core training products for the Center, including facilitator training, TQM management implementation training, executive quality leadership, and basic TQM tools training. In addition to developing these products, he has facilitated numerous improvement teams and has consulted with Asea-Brown-Boveri, the Central Intelligence Agency, and others in support of quality, productivity, and organizational improvement objectives. Mr. Beans is a member of the American Society for Quality Control, and he holds a B.A. degree in international relations and political science and an MPA, both from the University of South Carolina.

Debra L. Eshelman is an adult education specialist and has helped develop most of the Center for Excellence training materials. She has facilitated improvement teams and provided quality management training to executives, managers, and facilitators. As an adjunct professor at American University, she developed and taught "train-the-trainer" courses on adult learning theory and training design and evaluation. She has been certified as a professional by the Society for Human Resource Management, and is a member of the American Society for Training and Development. She co-authored an article on quality tools training in *Training,* and earned a B.A. degree in education at the University of Florida and an M.S. in human resource development at Virginia Polytechnic.

Index

abnormal distribution 79-80
abnormal variation 7, 73, 75-76, 87, 89, 91
act phase 9, 10, 142-150
action plan 123, 154
administrator 18
analytical tools 7
analyzer 16
average 57

bar charts 71-73, 155-156
barriers, removal of 145
bell-shaped curve 78-79
brainstorming 116, 157-159

c chart 85, 87, 89, 186-190
cause data 55-56
cause-and-effect diagrams 109-110, 160-162
cause-and-effect relationship 112-113
central tendency 78, 84
charter 30, 34
challenge assumptions 163-164
charting tools 71-73
check phase 9, 136-142, 144
checksheets 64-65, 165-166
code of conduct 26-28
conflict stage 25
consensus 13, 18-19
control charts
• c-chart 85, 87, 89, 186-190
• p-chart 85, 87, 180-185
• X and MR chart 85, 87, 89, 174-179
• X̄ and R chart 85, 87, 89, 167-173
control lines
• center line 83-84,90
• upper control limit 83-84, 87, 90

- lower control limit 83-84, 90

coordinator 13

cost-benefit analysis 121, 141

costs, estimating 141

customers
- external 4
- expectations 1, 2
- internal 4

creative thinking 19, 98

customer/manager interview 30, 37-44

data
- attribute 85, 87, 89
- cause 55-56
- existing 58-59
- new 58-59
- performance 45-46
- subgroups 59-62
- variable 85

data collection
- keys to successful 54
- types 55, 65-66, 103-104

deployment chart 32, 191-192

distribution
- abnormal 79
- bimodal 80
- bunched 80
- flat 80
- normal 78-79
- skewed 80

do phase 9, 131-134

evaluation tools 121

existing data 58-59

facilitator 18

flowcharts
- deployment 32, 191-192
- detailed 193-194
- top-down 31, 46, 71, 99, 228-229

force field analysis 120, 195-197

frequency distribution 57-58, 60, 77
frequency table 221

Gantt chart 123, 198-199
gatekeeper 14
group 24-27
groupthink 19, 20

harmonizer 14
histograms 71-73, 77-83, 200-202
home base 26

idea assassins 115
idealized redesign 118, 203-205
implementation schedule 123
implementation plan 135-136
implementator 16-17
in-control process 89-90
innovator 15-16
inputs 5, 33
interview
• assignments 42
• guidelines 41
• plan 37-42
intuitive techniques 118

leveraging improvement 150
logs 55

measurement 5-6, 47-49
measurement plan 6, 52-53, 66-67, 88-89, 138
measurement system 147-148
median 111, 200, 224-225
mode 78-79, 200
MR chart 85, 87, 89, 174-179
multi-voting 43, 122, 206

networker 13
new data 58-59
nominal group technique 207-208

normal curve 78-79
normal distribution 78-79

opportunity grid 43-44, 209-210
Osborn's brainstorming rules 116
output characteristics
- definition 49
- examples 50-52
outputs 5, 33
out-of-control process 89

p chart 85, 87, 180-185
pairwise ranking matrix 43, 122, 211-212
Pareto diagrams 71, 94, 108, 213-215
PDCA (plan-do-check-act cycle) 8, 9, 129-151
performance data 55-56
pie charts 71-73, 216-217
plan phase 8, 9
problem checklist 102-103
problem statement 100-102
process
- boundaries 31
- components 34, 61
- customers and managers 33
- definition 5, 29-30
- inputs 5, 33
- outputs 5, 33
- scope 35
- streamlining 105-106
process flow analysis 31-32, 93, 101-105

quality 1, 2

range 57, 167-172, 201, 221
ranking table 38
ranking tools, 121
review board 121, 218-220
root cause
- analysis 107-112
- definition 107
run charts 71, 73, 81-83, 221-222

sample size 62
sampling method 63
sampling table 63-64, 201-202
scatter diagrams 110-112, 223-225
shaper 15
solution maps 117, 226-227
standard deviation 84, 86
stratification 60-62
subgroups 59-62
suppliers 3-4
synergy 26
systematic diagram 230-231
systems 5

tables 71-72
team formation 8, 11-12, 24
team
• group dynamics 8, 12-14
• task roles 14-19
• team roles 17-18
top-down flowchart 31, 46, 71, 99, 228-229
TQM
• definition 2
• what's different under TQM 8
tree diagram 113-114, 230-231

variation
• abnormal 7, 73, 75-76, 87, 89, 91
• effects of 6-7, 74
• examples of 6-7, 76-77
• normal 7, 73, 75-76, 89

$\underline{X}$ and MR chart 85, 87, 89, 174-179
$\overline{X}$ and R chart 85, 87, 89, 167-173

NOTES

NOTES

NOTES